For you

I hope you
this, as much as I did
writing it.

— Nana Tea

TO GOD ALMIGHTY

ISBN(s) - 978-9988-3-7233-0

Cover by Reins Films

Illustrated and Layout Adkin Advertising

Edited by Gabriel Myers Hansen

Published by Penman Publishing Limited

Penmanonline.com

"My wonderful mother,

Like an onion, you experience the

knife to emit your unique aroma,

so your offspring could bask in a flavorful life."

– Your daughter.

Contents

MARGARET

Chapter 1
A cry from the beyond

If you're reading this, then I'm already dead. My body must have conceded in the prolonged battle with anxiety and chronic stress which, after a few years, had borne me the gift of type II diabetes. It was never a strategy to bow out of life this way, much less three days to my 59th birthday. But life happens as the Lord wills it. His ways are not our ways.

It was as the time I had awoken from the Caesarian section - like how we welcomed Obaapa, the youngest of my children, into the world. A temporal metallic taste of death in my mouth as I opened my eyes to the blur of life; again, it may have been an effect of the various anesthetics administered before the surgery. Thoughts of my readiness to risk it all to bear another child baffled my brother Kissi. His anger, coated with hints of love, was channelled through the many words he yelled out at my bedside at the Ridge Hospital in Accra. It was a high-risk pregnancy; diabetes had already set in to dehydrate what was left of the moisture in my body, my sugar levels skyrocketed and sent my body into some kind of shock at the labour ward.

Except for this time, consciousness was far from reach; the line between us displeasingly blurred. The plaintive cries of my daughters, oh how lovely they were, were the startling call to my new reality that I was out of this world and bound for my first trip on the spiritual plane. Ohemaa, my first daughter, was only 18 at the time and had to bear the responsibility of catering for my youngest, Obaapa. I watched as they both clung onto my lifeless body, bellowing out to me - a humble order to wake up. It hurt that I had not prepared them well enough for my exit and what to expect from the rest of the extended family now that I'm no more.

My name is Margaret Yaa Owusua Asare and you're welcome to call me Auntie Maggie as you read through the travails of my lifetime.

Charles Nelson Appiah 'Piesare' Asare, my father, was a cocoa farmer. He was a good man. Piesare was his moniker, one coined from a portmanteau of his surnames Appiah and Asare. He was a hard-working man who raised an average weekly income by buying and selling cocoa from local farmers within and around our village. Loving my mother was what he knew to do best besides farming. He adored his seeds, all six of us. Though he could not offer us the best education, he never fell short in equipping us with the right morals to walk upright in life. His go-to line was always to be content with what we had, *"Maw'ani nsɔ nea wo wɔ,"* he'd say after catching us salivating over the *akrantie* soup Maa Afia Fosua and her family enjoyed next door.

My father was a loving, kind man who at a point in our upbringing was rendered poor. He had fallen victim to a scam initiated by his nephew, Teacher Aninkora, one of the sons of his favourite sister, Kumiwaa. He had introduced some people to my unwitting father, claiming they could double his money. Papa wasn't greedy.

No. The old man had thought that Nananom had presented to him the opportunity to finally live a prosperous life and to cater for his family, in the best way a man should. "He who honours his ancestors is bound to receive their blessings," he began.

"Anin, *Awurade* de wo aba fie sɛ mendi yie. God has led you here to make me prosperous. You have done well for remembering your *akora*." Akora was the name Animkora had given to my father, which loosely translates to "old man".

"Oh akora, berima na ɛdi adepa ba fie o. It is the man who brings a good thing home. Immediately my people came in with the news, you came to mind."

Aninkora wore a yellow linen shirt over a pair of khaki trousers, and his people, the two strangers who had accompanied him, were finely dressed in matching black pants; one in a tie-dye shirt, the other in an overwashed white linen shirt. Papa had welcomed them on the weakly wooden bench which sat in the middle of our compound. The visitors were refreshed with water from the clay pot Mama had carried to their presence. Her dainty bare feet slapped the red earth as she dashed from the smoky *mukaase* with the pot, her *Afe Bi Yɛ Esan* cloth tied loosely around her waist. The water tasted like white clay, yet was deeply satisfying.

Something was unsettling about how Aninkora rattled; the descriptions of Akwasi broni, the white man, and how he had brought about this new money doubling scheme. Also, the way he lazily lifted his left arm to scratch his temple, revealing the unpleasant sight of a light brown singlet from the gaped sleeves of his shirt, in between his many lines, gave him away to me. The image of his singlet would play in my head for days after. I could swear it used to be white.

My nose twitched at the smell of lies in the air. It was unbearable. Even Kojo Kissi, the last of my siblings, could tell that something was amiss. It was definitely about the stories told by Aninkora and his matching trouser friends.

"Maggie, *ampa*?" he asked, pointing his chin towards the direction of the gathering.

"What?" I asked

"Do you believe what Aninkora is telling Papa?"

"Well, something seems off about his blabbering."

"Nti, why isn't Papa dismissing him? Look at how his eyes are widening in excitement."

Our father had failed to read between the lines. His trusting persona had become a weakness.

"I overheard Teacher Aninkora say, that if Papa invested as little as pesewa mmienu koraa, he would certainly get it back in double folds," I added.

"Hopefully, Papa will start small."

Sadly, he didn't. He went in big and lost it all. I believe his nephew had sealed the deal with him when he listed the many people whose lives had been enriched through the scheme - especially Kofi Mante of Osino, Akosua Dompreh of Mfante and Teacher Duah of Asaaman Tamfoe. You see, these were people from the neighbouring towns, whom we had heard had come into sudden wealth and were commanding exploits in the capital city, Accra. My Papa had a wife and six children to feed, and generational wealth to establish. He thought Aninkora could do him no wrong, He was family after all. It was Papa who had supported Kumiwaa at Aninkora's naming ceremony, so entrusting Aninkora with his earnings was easy.

Trust - it was the one thing I had picked up from Papa aside from his tiny pointy nose and thin ankles. It was what fueled his life of peace with himself and with others. The one thing I had admired about him had become his curse...even mine. The tension which hung over our home during the subsequent months was thick, you could slice it with a machete.

The news of the scam had spread through the huts in our village, Ankaase, where Opanyin Piesare, my Papa, was revered. Each day for one month, some villagers would come knocking to express their sympathy for Papa's misfortune. I counted close to 10 visitors, men and women, per day. To worsen his woes, some so-called sympathisers would furnish him with gossip about how Aninkora's entourage had fled the countryside after swindling Papa and a few others from neighbouring villages. Papa would respond with a sigh: "Hmm, m'ati. I've heard you, they should go with God." He was not the type to raise hell in any situation. He kept his composure and suffered the shame in silence.

Ours was a little village, with no more than 70 huts scattered in the middle of the rain forest beyond the River Birim, over a vast land we called Dadaso, which translates to, 'on the old place.' The young men of my village, mostly farmers and hunters, married from the neighbouring villages. There was Abompe to the East, Asaaman to the West, Osino to the north and Mfante to the south. As our population increased, so did the number of huts. The Amankrado, who was the head of the village, after deliberations with the elders and family heads including Papa, decided to move Ankaase closer to the inter-regional road networks and national routes constructed by the government to link Accra to the hinterlands between the late 1950s to the early 60s. A vast area was cleared and new homes constructed with clay blocks sprouted. Two of Papa's siblings chose an area close to Dada 'Obroni' Diyiifour the priest's plot, while other families scattered evenly over the vast open area. Ankaase moved from Dadaso to its current location to be properly sandwiched by Osino and Asaaman Tamfoe. The village had finally become a visible part of the Fanteakwa district and a small chain of government schools in shabby buildings erupted at its entrance. I found it interesting how our elders had cut out the village like a big compound house; with a single entrance and exit by the main Accra-Kumasi Road, with the inner river-farm routes serving as some sort of emergency exit.

Our new home was built with blocks from clay, plastered with mud and coated with whitewash paint. It stood immaculately in the middle of the village. Ten feet away from the village center which housed the little market square where the women sold foodstuff and other farm produce. The young women sold smoked catfish and akrantie, harvested from the Birim and hunted in the forest respectively. The early to middle 60s opened our village to various imported goods from Accra and the West. Canned sardines, tuna, cocoa powder, corned beef and more freely circulated in our village. Our new location afforded the women the opportunity to travel to bigger, eastern towns like Tafo and Koforidua, to trade in these commodities at their huge market squares. Mama was not among them. She worked along with Papa on our cocoa and plantain farm by the Birim River. Despite the mishap, she had continued to stand by him, at least for the first few years, until she had abandoned the struggle to begin a new life elsewhere without Papa. You see, in the typical tale of poverty and its accompanying shame, one can only take so much. Unable to bear the humiliation that had been bestowed upon the family; she separated from Papa and relocated to her maternal home in Jejeti. I was about eleven years old.

Maame Sarah 'Saara' Agyeiwaa Nyarko, my mother, was a quiet one who only revealed a sharp tongue when provoked. Whenever we failed to adhere to her instructions, she would throw a fit of irritation and extend that with the silent treatment for the rest of the day. Peace of mind was Mama's topmost priority and due to this, she did well to avoid gatherings of notable village gossipmongers, especially in places where Otema Ayisi dared to show her face. Otema was the village gossip queen. If one needed damning details about another or the latest happenings behind the clay walls of any Ankaase natives, she was the one to call. Mama had an average build - about 5.6 feet - and her skin was enriched with plentiful melanin.

Mama's father, Opanyin Nyarko, had named her Saara, per the custom of their tribe. At that time, when a couple lost more than a child successively, they were required by the nananom to give the next one some sort of comical name to repel the baby-reaping demons.

To the best of my knowledge, she had loved Papa. I'm compelled to believe that she had done everything within her charm as a woman, to hinder his plans of investing all of his savings. Knowing my father and his nature of persistence, I had come to understand that, no amount of coercion from Mama could have sullied what he had termed, his 'divine moment of breakthrough.' Whatever Mama's sentiments, she ensured to air them out behind the curtain of their wooden door frame. I once saw him lean against the black smoked wall of our open clay kitchen, next to the *mukyia* - the three mounds of red earth on which we cooked, optimism deserted me. His faded cloth hung carelessly around his skinny waist revealing a visibly ribbed torso. He whispered a silent prayer to *Nyankopon,* our Heavenly Father, and nananom to let favour smile upon him once more by bringing his wife back, dashing all hopes I harboured about Papa regaining his normalcy. Like me, he tended to obsess over a situation till it became all he could see. The swindle made him sick, a little too slow, and Mama's absence had snuffed out his essence, placing him under a dark cloud.

From the mid-1960s my village had a single thriving church; the very one I believe, the Presbyterian missionaries had left behind. It had existed under a copse of neem trees at Dadaso. Dada Diyiifour, the overseer of the church, continued to head the church after assuming the position at age nineteen. We gave him the moniker 'Obroni' because of his fired-clay complexion. On certain days, he appeared as yellow as the sun or as white as the white man.

We continued Mama's tradition of rising before the cock's crow on Sundays to carry out our assigned chores before church service. The auditorium stood beyond a thicket of plantain and lemon trees, 20 feet away from our home. The routine was simple; we fetched water from the black barrels placed in all four corners of our house, to scrub and bathe with. We had always made sure to fill the barrels to the brim after our many trips to the riverside.

Auntie Abena Fofie sold porridge from one of the many wobbly wooden stands next to the market square. I had particularly grown fond of her corn dough porridge with the *whentea* spice, locally known as "koko". We made similar breakfast at home on a few Sundays but the taste could not compare to that of Auntie Fofie. Even wives, with their husbands in tow, would rush to the market square to get a bowl of her porridge.

"Fofie, won't you share with us the secret potion you've been adding to your koko? One woman asked.

"Ah! She won't o, I've been asking for almost a year now." Another retorted.

"Awura, I may have to kill you if I tell you o. *Na,* how will I continue to make a profit if I share with everyone my recipe?" Auntie Fofie answered with a smile. There was something about how she meticulously arranged the *whentea* in the bowl before pouring in the porridge. It reflected a silent thoughtfulness, which was indeed typical of most Ankaase natives.

Honestly, our Sundays were unwholesome without breakfast from Fofie. Coupled with the fog and cold air, it felt like paradise.

I would walk briskly home before the bell ringer would come to sound the hollow metallic doobry, releasing an irritating toll summoning us to church. He always struck in a familiar rhythm: *gban-gban gban- gban,* repeatedly until he saw some villagers walking towards the premises.

Papa would peer into our eyes when we took time to get ready for church as if the auditorium would be filled if we didn't make haste. It wasn't our fault. It was Auntie Fofie's porridge. It was bound to make you sluggish after consumption; yet, it remained our Sunday go-to. A tasty addiction.

Adwoa 'ayo' Afumaa, the third of my siblings took a strange liking to church activities. She grew closer to Dada Diyiifour and eventually became a vibrant part of the Presbyterian Young People's Guild. There were six of us - my father's children: three males and three females. There was Teacher Kwadwo Agyei, Felicia Yaa Anima, Adwoa Ayo Afumaa, Teacher Stephen Yaw Asare, Margaret Yaa Owusua and Ransford Kwadwo Kissi Appiah. The first four of the six had a three-year age gap. The last two, my brother and I, were born four years apart.

The church had no microphones or keyboards. We used tambourines and drums covered with cow skin in our joyful noises to God. The church owned two megaphones which were only used for external evangelism. Though the Akosombo dam had been constructed, electricity had not properly made its way into our village; a scattered flicker of light bulbs illuminated ten houses at night.

Diyiifour, in an oversized pantsuit, would shout out sermons to the hearing of passersby who leisurely walked outside the auditorium. While my ears listened, my eyes were fixated on the tight veins which bulged under the skin of his neck. He was light-skinned with thick jerry curls, which sparkled under the sun's rays. It looked as though he had used an entire bottle of palm kernel oil to maintain its shine. His sons, Kweku Tui and Agyebeng rocked the jerry curls too. This, I had come to notice after our village's relocation. Our nearness to the major Eastern inter-regional roads had awarded the village folks a sense of civilisation, I thought.

Sermons on love and forgiveness were jewels in the crown of Dada Diyiifour. He would add new twists to previous sermons on the same topic each week. Instead of paying attention to the message from the altar, I would look out for familiar lines for my pleasure. I suspect that when the *"Yɔnko dɔ oo, biako yɛ"* greeting, which translates to "love one another, there's good in unity," was coined, the priest had a hand in it. Thus was the situation in Ankaase; everyone knew and loved one another. It was a mass gathering whenever a member of the village journeyed to the land of the ancestors. The women in the village would automatically assume kitchen duties in the compound of the bereaved. The men would bring *nsafufuo* in kegs, along with bush meat; notable of them, the *akrantie* and *kusie*. With his greasy black jerry curls, Dada Diyiifour would grace the occasion with sermons again on love. This time, it was regarding how God had loved the departed so much that, He had forgiven and granted them rest in the bosom of Abraham. This was mostly followed by long hymns and wails as the air continued to possess the aroma of smoked bush meat, *akpeteshie* gin and light soup.

Sundays were joyous for Papa; he had found solace in the house of God. He would wrap his slender frame in one of the few good pieces of cloth he had left, often pairing it with a pair of *ahenema* slippers. Despite his heartbreak and financial instability, he had held high his hopes. "*Na anidaso ɔ nhyɛ aniwuo*...Hope maketh not ashamed," he once quoted Romans 5:5 for consolation.

Chapter 2

Trails and bloodlines

Exogamy accounted for the rapid population growth in our village. Strangers from far lands and ethnicities, who had poured into our village to trade, ended up marrying our people. The unspoken rivalry between certain ethnic groups in Ghana had existed decades before I was born.

These constant squabbles, often clouded by irrational discriminatory statements, surrounded one party's claim of superiority over the other, or one pointing fingers at the other for growing an attachment to juju practitioners. Such was the story between the Akans; comprising Asantefuo, Akyemfuo, and Fantefuo, and the Ewes, all upholding chucklesome stories about one another. However, I had grown to understand that, it was merely a transient symptom because we, by default, sought ways to co-exist in harmony despite our perceptions regarding one another.

When several Ewes migrated to Ankaase, our elders allotted a vast land around the portion given to the Fantes, across the main road. The Ewe men soon penetrated the dense, Akyem-populated main Ankaase village, initially to work and later to woo and have children with our women. They worked hard at whatever occupation they laid hands on –

an attribute I believe attracted our ladies to them. We had neither a sawmill timber processing facility to process logs to lumber, but these *'anwonafuo'* as we had addressed them, were smart enough to have identified this problem and fashioned an ingenious but tedious means of wood processing. Their sense of reasoning and creativity was fascinating. I found remarkable the skill exhibited in the way they fell trees and prepared for processing. They dug two shallow pits on opposite sides, in which two smaller logs were placed. These men would then place the main trunk on top of the logged pits and saw it into marketable sizes. As the village expanded, so did their business - it became lucrative. People stormed the forest wood market to purchase lumber for their construction.

Every evening, the Ewes, after their evening meal, would visit my old man. He'd walk them to the mango tree behind our home, beneath which they'd sit to discuss a roll of topics I never fully understood. Papa, in his contributions, showcased immense wisdom. He appeared to me, in those moments, as a man of mystery - like an ancestor who had returned to his kinsmen to unravel mysteries from the beyond. His sermonised often, on the story of the female apparition whose home was in the Birim River, which was terrifying yet weirdly fascinating. It was said that the river goddess had the same complexion as the white man, with hair like silk running down to her buttocks. It was believed that she was married to the Pra river god and had bore five children with him. Birim Nana, so she was called, would take up full human form whenever she desired to visit market squares in all of the Akyem areas her home streamed through. Birim Nana was gifted in height - her feminine features pleasing to the eye. It was said that the fisherman who had dared to fish with chemicals was visited by the goddess in the dream world at night. The perpetrators either perished in their sleep or arose from their slumber blind. Stories were told of a middle-aged woman, Maame Pokuaa, also Mama's confidante, as the only person permitted to see the goddess at all times without repercussions. I hadn't thought much of her but I knew she was a strange one. Only she had been to the riverside on Tuesdays when it was forbidden.

Papa spoke in an unfamiliar tone with his eyes in a deep set gaze, the rest of his body sat frozen as his lips moved softly with every word. My father had revealed to me that night, followed by others, a spiritually inclined side of him I had previously not met. The wild exclamations and thunderous claps that followed his deliveries were signs that the gathering had been fully immersed in those moments under the mango tree.

I barely had a wink of sleep on many of those nights, often haunted by visions of Papa in a cloud of mist, surrounded by traditionally adorned people with bold *hyire* designs on their faces. They chanted gibberish and hopped from one end to the other, amidst various grotesque figures. My little brain had gone berserk with what I had come to believe represented Papa - the version of him beneath the mango tree.

One such evening, the gathering was unusual. Ransford sat at the feet of Papa, me leaning against the wall to hear what Papa had in store for the night, as we awaited that night's batch of listeners.

Then came a roar - a blend of drumming, hails and singing a complete tumult. "*Na* what's all that?" Papa asked peering into the darkness. The sun had set two hours earlier and the sky had given off its grayish hue to usher in the night sky. As the noise drew nearer, a group of young men and women wielding *bobo* tin lanterns appeared from the sharp curve adjacent to Maame Pokuwaa's window three feet away from the mango tree.

As they drew closer, Papa identified the leader. It was Edem - one of the Ewe lumbermen of Ankaase.

"Opanyin Piesare," he started, addressing my Papa.

"We have found one of our own."

"Your own?" My father inquired.

"Opanyin, this village has already given us so much. *ɛnɛ deɛ*, it has retraced our steps to a lost tribesman.

"Edem, can you hit the nail on the head already? Sitting in suspense is not my forte." Papa queried further, his brows furrowed in perplexity.

Here's the back story: in the olden days, when people would go to war over everything - mostly land, the Akyems in the late 1870s waged a war against the people of Botoku in the Volta Region of Ghana. As arrows flew, an Akyem warrior spotted a fair maiden with a waist heavily bedecked with clay beads. In the Ghanaian tradition, beads were a sign of beauty and fertility, to some, it was a catcall to pleasure. Together with the spoils of the conquest they had laid hands on, the fair maiden was brought to Ankaase Dadaso to live as the wife of her capturer. Other women were brought along with the fair maiden from Botoku, all of whom were married off to their captors. The maiden, called Dede, had a daughter named Kesiwaa, who happened to be my father's mother. In the Bible, this story of my heritage would have been written like the genealogy in Matthew 1:1-25. So, in our case; Dede begat Kesiwaa, Kesiwaa begat Piesare, Piesare begat Margaret, and so on.

We saw our grandmother, Nana Kesiwaa, briefly before her passing in the late 1960s. Like her mother, she was fair to gaze upon. Papa had four siblings, all of whom were illiterates and small-scale farmers. Papa was among the few who had hopped on the adult education wagon with what was left from the proceeds of his cocoa farming at the new Ankaase, to learn how to read and write. He was the *akurase krakye* who, with the knowledge acquired from the Adult in education studies, became the unofficial Birth registrar of our little village - we grew up having a notebook in our home which contained the dates of birth of almost everyone born in Ankaase. When people received letters, they would come to Papa to read them out and explain to them.

So, we had come to understand that Edem and his entourage had found out through the many stories told by Papa under the mango tree that they had come from the same town as Awo Dede, my great-grandmother, and were somehow related by blood. One would think that identity would not mean so much to a man who had gone farther in age, but Papa upon the revelation was fully immersed in the joyous atmosphere – I had not seen him this ecstatic in a long time.

. . .

When Mama relocated to her family home in Jejeti, her children chose to stay behind with our old man in Ankaase. I was ten years old and in Primary 5, while Ransford was just about to be enrolled in Primary 1. He was four years behind me in age. Our village was quite 'young' in the 1960's. Though blessed with a primary school by the Akyem council, the absence of a middle school brought a halt to whatever academic ambition we had silently nurtured. Papa, given this, had sent me off to live with Mama in Jejeti, where there were a handful of middle schools. Undeterred by his parents' inability to afford him an education or his financial woes, my father gave all he could to give us a certain level of education which could fit us into the new emerging world. Our country had become a republic and our father had envisioned a dignified place for us in it. Getting their children into the government middle schools (we called them *site-to)* in bigger neighbouring towns had become a prayer point for farmers and traders who had shared in the hopes of Papa. Life for Mama in Jejeti was not the kind she had hoped for. In her parent's *abusuafie,* there was no room for her. So, while we stayed with Papa in our own house in Ankaase, our mother sadly resorted to renting rooms wherever she could find in Jejeti. Could she have retraced her steps back to Papa? Yes, but the taste of poverty was like a mouthful of sand – tasteless and hard to swallow. Mama had wanted no part in that life. The schools in Jejeti were different, the classrooms were wider, the teachers more refined and the students, more welcoming than I had expected. Mama was her usual introverted self; she always kept to herself after farming without mingling with the women of the town. Unlike Papa, she didn't care about getting along with the townsfolk or being in their good books. Mama was an incredible cook, an attribute Papa had missed terribly in her absence. All the *mpotormpoto, apapransa, abɛ nkwan, abunuabunu* among other delicacies Ransford would grow to appreciate me for, were passed down to me by Mama. Even her neighbours could differentiate by the aroma when

Mama and others cooked. While the natives depended on stock cubes, Mama would simply, without struggle, fill her soup pot with blends of ginger, garlic, *nketenkete, ɛsuro wisa* which emitted the right amount of natural flavouring for her meals. This had caught the attention of Ampofo, who always called on Mama at home at odd hours. As if pressed for time, he would walk briskly into the compound, dragging his heavy feet in the process.

"Saara, nti wompene mma me ne wo ntena?"? *erh*? I'll take very good care of you." I had overheard him say one evening. Mama's door was made of very light wood. You could easily, without paying attention, overhear others' conversations from start to finish. Ampofo's intentions were not lost on me. I wasn't too naïve to fathom that he had wanted to replace Papa unofficially. Mama's night giggles with that man terrified me; the taciturn spinster had found her voice in what had appeared to be my worst nightmare. Spending my formative years in a broken home was already too much to bear, so, the last thing I wanted was to play a silent role in Mama's game of "match-me-please." I had known that the picture would have been enough reason to drag Papa back into the emotional black hole he had managed to wriggle out of.

"How selfish of her!" I blurted out to Ransford after he had joined me in Jejeti for his middle school education. I was a senior awaiting graduation. At only eleven years old, Ransford was quite the conversationalist.

"Who?"

"Mama, I can't believe she wants to replace Papa with that dimwit Ampofo."

"Maggie, why do you seem this troubled about this man? Besides, he's as old as Papa, why hurl insults at him? If he makes Mama happy…"

"Happy?" I interrupted. "What makes you think she is happy?"

"Then why the trigger?"

"Answer me this Kissi, would you rather not have a stable family where your parents co-existed in harmony?"

"Yes but why stir the muddy water? Why not give it all to time to settle?"

"Time would have done something for these two if it had wanted to."

"Well, this matter is beyond our control. They are adults and adults tend to do what they want."

"Can't we do…"

"Let this one rest Maggie." He answered with his right palm lifted as a signal to halt.

"*Mati wai.*" I finally said in surrender.

Ransford was right, it was beyond my control. I had failed to read that, it was unlike high school relationships where one could intervene and pull certain strings to manipulate it towards an expected end. Prior to moving in with me and Mama at Jejeti, my brother had spent vacations several vacations from Ankaase's primary school with us. Those years had nurtured our enviable bond and had made us inseparable. I say enviable because, while we had much older siblings, our relationships with them were very much awkward. Of course, they noticed how Kissi and I giggled and took several walks to the river to wash our clothes. Where you saw one, you found the other. By the time Afumaa, Maa Yaa and the others had wanted to catch on with our bond, we had gone farther and had grown stronger.

I had turned sixteen after graduating from Jejeti Methodist Middle School. I had hoped to pursue a college education from there but neither Papa nor Mama was financially capable of pushing me up that ladder. My mother, aside from supporting Kissi with her meagre earnings, had spent a chunk of it renting rooms in the compounds of whoever would let her. The landlords of Jejeti were brutal in the pricing of their homes and that pushed Mama from one home to the other. It was such that, by the time I completed middle school, we had moved into about five different compounds. The logical thing to do in my case was to either learn a trade or get a job. The latter seemed more reasonable than the former. So with the little I had saved and what Mama had been able to support with from selling produce from her farm, I prepared to depart to Nkawkaw in search of a job and a means to a better life. It had appeared to me at the time, the only way to save up towards a higher education.

The mammy trucks and lorries which plied the Osino-Nkawkaw road had only operated between the hours of 5 am and midday. If one needed to travel to Nkawkaw and other regional towns without succumbing to the ridiculous demands of the Datsun 240z taxi drivers; who charged desperate passengers exorbitant fees on their journey, then it was important to factor in the operating hours in one's itinerary.

I sat at the edge of my seat, counting down the minutes until descent. I had been pushed against the glassless window by the large *kɛntɛn,* a traditional woven basket, of a market woman. It carried an assortment of smoked and dried fishes, predominant among them; *momone* and *kako.* The pungent smell from her basket had completely submerged the fragrance of my midnight talcum powder. Looking through the glassless window, away from the suffocating smell, I relived moments spent with Papa and Mama, both together and apart.

Travelling by road in the pre-mobile phone era, the luxury of wiping out boredom, by simply scrolling for minutes on end on social media for a good laugh was absent. However, the heavy inscriptions behind various trucks, lorries and *trotros,* served as good entertainment or a distraction from a bumpy ride. Some of the aphorisms read: "FEAR WOMEN, OH!" "MY WIFE, LIFE IS SHORT", "THIS TOO SHALL

PASS", "DUA KORO GYE MFRAMMA A EBU" and "SIKA MPɛ DEDE" which implied "a single tree which faces the storm would break," and "money does not like noise" respectively. These writings came often in giant multicoloured fonts or ridiculous bold italics.

Nkawkaw, the district capital of Kwahu East Municipality, sits at the foot of the Kwahu Mountains. It is described as the gateway to the popular town, which is revered for its rich tradition and in the present times, its exaggerated and urbanised Easter festivities.

Their multi-business activities certainly make it the little Accra of the Eastern Region. I found myself a home in this place in early 1966. In less than a week I had managed to secure a spot at Kwahu Laundries, a popular cleaning company within the district, as a supervisor/records keeper. As with the beginning of every new phase, there are the jitters which leave one with fear of whether what was to begin is what should be. I suffered a slight anxiety attack on my way to work the first time. My sweaty feet slid out a few times from my Kumasi slippers. My heart skipped a few beats, my lips appeared dehydrated beneath two coats of brown lipstick and my stomach rumbled, creating excess gas which had failed to pass with ease. The conspicuous Nkawkaw laundries Company sign, towered above the many signboards sprawling on the borders of the roads. Painted beneath the writing was a big green arrow, pointing towards the direction of the business. The 'y' at the end of 'company' appeared faint, making it read 'Nkawkaw Laundries Compan' rather than 'Company', which had given me a good laugh, allaying my fears.

My assigned post required that I make both mental and written notes of payments and services rendered. I did, without struggle, my supervisory duties - reporting an hour before the work began and seeing to it that our industrial-sized washing machines were turned on at the commencement of every shift and off at the end. In other words, I had been the very soul upon which the business had come to operate. My flair for the Queen's language had made me the mouthpiece of the boss', when we were to bid for the contracts to carry out laundry services for large companies, my boss would say,

"*Yaa Maggie, sɛ wo wie sukuu nkyɛ yɛ,* go and demonstrate your command over the *brofo kasa,* so these people would come to know that this isn't one of those regular local businesses."

Brofo kasa loosely translates as "English language". For some reason, the people I had worked with, even the ones who had been gracious enough to have let out a single room to me, two hours upon arrival in the town, had seemed to have found me a rarity. I had thought it to be due to my young petite stature, my upright morals or perhaps my smile. Looking back I see, without a streak of doubt that it had been the favour of God at work upon me. Occasionally, mostly on Easter and on Christmas, I'd visit Mama and Kissi at Jejeti with goodies of the season. If I had a week to spare, I'd stay three days with Mama then journey by *trotro* for thirty minutes to Ankaase to be with my old man for three more days. Papa appeared feeble, more due to internal agony than age. It had been five years since the separation yet each passing year had magnified his pain. Absence does make the heart grow fonder.

Two years at Nkawkaw and I was already hungry. An insatiable desire to earn more had cajoled me into making the bold move to be a part of the increasing statistics of rural-urban migration. Mama had recounted stories of young men and women from Jejeti who had fled from the hinterlands in search of greener pastures in the city. Moreover, I had learnt from reading several newspapers that, the city held the best schools in the country. What more did a girl need? I had asked myself? My ambitions were limitless; I had envisioned working a steady job while studying for a professional credential. Driven by Academic curiosity and a quest for financial freedom, I bid farewell to Nkawkaw and headed back to Mama's town.

"Ampadu ne Gifty have also fled Jejeti." She had begun after serving me a portion of *fufu* and *amane nkwan* she had prepared earlier.

"They have managed to secure jobs in city. Gifty serves as an assistant to a wealthy second-hand trader, and Ampadu drives one of the new sprinter *trotro.*"

"So what happened to their education? *WƆn nkƆ sukuu biom anaa?*" I quizzed with concern.

"Yaa paa, we're talking money here and you're preaching education. For Ampadu, I'm sure he will find himself back in academic pursuit after he has had enough saved and found himself a nice lady."

"And Gifty? She was the brightest student from my graduation year, my one worthy contender in the English language class. Will Aunty Bea, her mother, see it all wither away?" I had asked, throwing my lightweight on a bench with a bowl of *fufu* well balanced in my left palm.

"Maggie," Mama said, settling on a wooden stool beside me, "you see, No matter how high the ladder of education a woman may climb, she is bound to end up in the kitchen of a man."

"Eii!" I exclaimed. My mouth gaped and right arm froze in a bend. The ball of fufu failed to go down with a single gulp.

Mama had preached inferiority; she had blasphemed against all women. What about all Dr. Kwegyir Aggrey, had said, about how a nation is educated if women were given a fair chance at it? It was March 1973 and Mama had still not disposed of the obsolete perceptions of the 1930s and 1800s. Undeterred, I packed my luggage and set out to begin a whole new life in Accra. Not without seeing my old man, I thought that he'd have some gems to share for the voyage ahead and I was right. Two days had turned into a week with Papa, he still spent leisure under the mango tree on weekends.

I had badly wanted to initiate a similar bond I had shared with Kissi with my two older sisters. Since he had completed his middle school education, Kissi now shuffled between Jejeti and Ankaase; Sometimes travelling the hinterlands to live with our older brother, Yaw Asare, in Wenchi. Maa Yaa and Ayo Afumaa had a sisterhood, which I believe was created on a shared notion of seniority over the last three of us. They were *mpanyinsem* and often discussed topics lost on me… It had grieved me that I did not feel acquainted with the other two females of my siblings. It was up to me to make my final nights in Ankaase before my departure count. So, when Maa Yaa, the oldest of us three, had asked me to accompany them to the dance at the village square adjacent to the main road, I was over the moon. My cravings for a place in the sisterhood, I believe, were fueled by fear - fear of missing out, fear of being isolated from what was left of the Asare family. They had after all spent more time together alone than ever did with them. Mama had taken half our identity with her, and somehow I had felt a silent burden to keep the rest family together by any means necessary.

The village dance was held twice on weekends every month. It saw a gathering of youthfulness and bloom - Young men and women, standing in a wide circle with sound speakers, made of wood and metal mesh, erect at the centre of the gathering. It played

hot high life and Ghanaian funk tunes of the 70s, which had invoked the waist of young ladies into a rhythmic twist. Amponsah was the Michael Jackson of Ankaase. He was sophisticated, and the only young man from our village who had owned a ghetto blaster. Paired with Agya Kusi's wooden speakers, it had summoned a party. He wore his hair in jerry curls like Dada Diyiifour; he had skin like red earth and the height of a long fufu pestle. He, like the handful of ambitious lads in our village, had gone to the city in search of a better life. Auntie Connie, his mother, had revealed to Papa that, Amponsah was a successful *trotro* conductor in the city. I wore a blue thin strapped top over a white pleated skirt. To shield myself from the night's cold, I threw a thick camo scarf I had bought from Nkawkaw market over my shoulders. My sisters wore matching black skirts. Maa Yaa in a brown *obroni wawu* sequin top, Afumaa in a yellow printed t-shirt with bluebird *chalewote*.
We danced to tunes from CK Mann, Gyedu Blay Ambolley, Ebo Taylor and the Apagya Show Band. Felt like my very own send-off party to Accra.

The dance had eaten the night away. It was past midnight and the gathering had begun to disperse. My sisters and I had realised how late it had gotten when the chirps of the crickets grew louder with each step. We had happened to be the only people on the single path.

"The *osram* is full; it must be the end of the month already," I said in an attempt to break the awkward silence. The moon was glorious. It was indeed full and showcased its beauty in the well-lit sky. A deep stare at it, I swore a man stood with his arms high ready to beat the two drums before him. From another twisted neck angle, Mary sat with grace holding and doting on baby Yesu Christo.

"Ah yes! It is." said Maa Yaa "uhuh! Maggie, when do you journey for the city?"

"In three days Maa, I would have left already if not for Papa. He insists on soaking in more time with me."

"Papa *dierr saa na Ɔteɛ*. Just do well to leave as early as possible, who knows what opportunities you might be missing out on."

"True, I'll go with Papa to the farm tomorrow to fetch some yams and cocoyam for the journey."

"Aunty Oglo came by earlier with some *adwene* and dried bush meat for Papa, you should take a portion with you as well, at least to keep you nourished till you get a job." Added Afumaa.

Our conversations were often distracted by our own footsteps against the gravelled road. It had stirred up a feeling, as though there was a fourth presence. The moon had cast hopping silhouettes of our frames before us. One, two, three and more fireflies danced their glowing bottoms in the bushes.

"Ah look at that firefly," I said pointing ahead. It was immobile in mid-air. As we drew closer, the tiny sparkle of what I had assumed was a firefly grew into the size of a tennis ball. We paused for evaluation.

"Afumaa can a firefly grow this big?" Maa Yaa wondered, her shaky voice unveiling her fears. The fireball stood about six feet farther. We took three more steps towards the object; it was after all, in our way. The glistening celestial body, appearing aggravated by our audacity to come an inch closer, grew the size of a football. This is no fiction, it had happened before my very eyes. I saw my sisters disappear into the bushes. Optimism deserted me, I took to my heels and miraculously found myself at home in minutes. Visibly shaken by whatever had transpired, I hugged the bare earth and lay frozen. My sisters arrived moments later. Maa Yaa, like me, was overcome with many emotions. Our eyes communicated each other's fears and questions.

"If that thing had followed us home, I would have shown it who's boss. It would have witnessed me transform into a tigress to fight it ah!" Afumaa said jumping on her toes from one end to the other.

"My friend quit with the useless brag, you might wake Papa. Why were you unable to display your prowess out there at that thing?" said Maa Yaa. I slowly crawled my way into our shared room, replaying the bizarre moment in my mind. What might that have been?

Chapter 3

From Accra with love

Bubiashie, one of the suburbs of Greater Accra; was nothing like Nkawkaw, Jejeti or Ankaase. This was a highly sophisticated town crammed with robust enterprises on every street. Kumaa, a gracious soul I was blessed to have crossed paths with in Nkawkaw, had agreed to accommodate me in the chamber-and-hall room she had rented on a compound house. The building had reminded me of the coop Papa had built for his fowls - Almost life-sized and boxy with individual compartments, guarded by a spacious play area for the fowls to freely tread about. It had been as a result of a hobby he had picked from spending time with the Ewe lumbermen. There was the desperation to fill out the long hours of empty silences which lingered after he had returned from working on the farm, where songs from his blade-cutting foliage had occupied his thoughts.

As an excuse he would say, "The devil finds work for the idle hands so to keep him at bay, I have to keep busy." But I knew - we all knew that it had been a ruse to flee his painful thoughts.

In a week, with guidance from Kumaa, I gained employment with Hope Paper Products, a manufacturing company which converted papers into envelopes, exercise books, paper bags etc. I was enrolled as a floor assistant on the production team, which implied that I showed up at work an hour before the scheduled opening time. Though tedious, I had taken pride in knowing that at only age nineteen I was halfway to becoming a financially independent woman. I secured a large single room in house number forty-five, about two buildings away from Kumaa's residence. I recall her reluctance to have me move out.

"Yaa, why don't you stay longer eh? Now that you have a job you want to leave me."

"Oh Kumaa it's not that oh you see; they say that house guests are like carcasses, they stink after three days. I have overstayed my welcome, my sister."

"And who had it bothered?" she had quickly interrupted, sucking air between her teeth. "We could split the cost you know."

"What cost?"

"The rent! You stay here and at the end of every month, we'll split the bill."

"That's not a bad idea. I'll even get to save more money but answer me this, how long do you intend to keep me out on the porch whenever Nkrumah makes one of his late-night appearances?"

That had her tongue tied up for a good minute. Nkrumah was her bald beau. "The one" that according to her had checked off every item on her list. I had respectfully excused myself from the living room after Kumah had burst into soft moans on the sofa on one of Nkrumah's random visits. It had escaped their thoughts for a moment that there had been a third party present.

"Well," she had resumed after the pause.

"If you insist, that's fine, however, do well to stop by at any time."

"But not without my cow leg palm nut soup right?"

"You already know. I'm appeased now"

We laughed for a long time about that.

I had noticed his stares - Gottfried Kofi Kwaakye, whenever he came past my workplace. He drove a fairly used Land Rover which he was rumored to have inherited from his father. He'd often slow down or park two shops away, to just walk over to Hope Paper products to make an enquiry we knew he'd never follow through with. My boss fell for it the first time, but when Gottfried had failed to define his enquiry on his countless subsequent visits, he had come to know that his visits were centred on matters of the heart.

"Maggie, your boyfriend awaits." He said gesturing to the silver car parked outside the shop.

"My boyfriend?" I asked feigning ignorance.

"Do you think he merely enjoys going on casual drives or senselessly stopping by paper shops to stutter meaningless words?" he was right, I had questioned his motives earlier - his awkward winks and direct grins.

He honked, peering through the cloudy windshield, as one would summon a hastening hawker. "Bra Gottfried *mmom dierr* oh! So he expects me to walk out of the shop, as though, we have an understanding? *Hoh.*" I was stunned by his audacity, displeased even, yet a part of me had secretly hoped that he'd walk into the shop to properly woo me. I believed the angel of romance was up to a good thing when Gottfried entered the shop.

"Yaa Owusua," addressing me by my maiden name, "a word please?" my eyes met his gaze. A man must be ugly and fearful they say, but this one's features were pleasing to the eye. He had the stature of a giant with a caramel complexion. To determine a man's level of hygiene, I'd focus on how well he groomed his feet and most importantly the colour of the spaces between the rows of his teeth. His sandals revealed a set of beautiful toes and well-groomed nails. He displayed a healthy set of teeth which glistened in the sun while we spoke.

"Can I take you out tonight? I get off work early on erm Fri-Fridays and would be honored to buy you a drink or di-dinner."

"Relax Kofi," I said touching the tip of his bent elbow. I couldn't bear to see him further humiliate himself with those unmanly stutters. In about five minutes, I came to know that he worked as a secretary with the Ghana Broadcasting Corporation (GBC) and a tenant over at house number forty-seven, closer to Kumaa's residence than mine.

"I NEVER KNEW THAT GAs made soups like these. This light soup breathes home." Kofi, surprisingly undaunted by my harmless ethnocentrism, wagged his head and crowned it with a short laugh. He had picked me up from work for our very first date - not as a couple but as the kind which eases into the first stage of proper dating.

Mman Tee 'Hot' Restaurant, was the 'it place' for young couples at the time. Situated between Darkumanan and Odorkor, its regular customers swarmed from far distances. It was all Kumaa talked about in my days of squatting at her residence. Nkansah, her bald beau, had taken her severally to the hot place. It was always "Nkansah this," "Nkansah that," various savoured versions of a single story - that her man was a big spender. My friend was the fabricator, I recall her narrations about how Gyedu Blay Ambulley winked at her at her gathering and about how she brushed him off after he had pursued her for an address. There's another version of this story where the *borga* highlife star called her up on stage to share a dance at a private event. One thing remained a mystery, she had failed to share with her many listeners, whose private event she had encountered the musician. Yet another was clear, Kumaa with her wild imagination was a great storyteller; a reason accounting for my disbelief when she shared the many tales of the out-of-this-world delicacies shared at Mman Tee.

"It's tacky- the name, too tacky," I said to Kumaa. "And what does 'Hot restaurant' even mean?"

"Perhaps it's about temperature... oh! Or even spice."

"I've had it with some of these Ga people oh. Too crass."

"*Hei* Yaa Maggie!" she exclaimed, jumping out of the cheaply cushioned chair to shut the wooden windows. "Are you trying to get me kicked out? My landlord is from Jamestown. *nwobenya asem* o, you'll get into trouble one of these days and I would not be there to help you."

To the middle class, Mman Tee was simply the plush place to treat oneself after a pressured week, to them it screamed a comfortable status in life and to the little-to-no earner, a wishful thought.

Kofi's laugh over my comment was a relief. It released him from the rigid perception I held of him. He wore a green long-sleeved shirt stiff with starch, a pair of brown khaki trousers and a black belt to match his greased leather shoes. His hair in a juice box fade haircut had a little shine to it – an indication of effort towards appearing impressive.

"I come here with the guys thrice a month for lunch." He said, interrupting my mental scrutiny of him.

"Thrice a month?" I asked with a giggle. "Is it to not permit your taste buds to get all too familiar?"

"Exactly!"

There was an easiness to his laughter that made me settle deeply into the plastic chair. This was home, he was home. We had spent hours at the hot restaurant. Then it dawned on me that, perhaps they had derived the name from its daily atmosphere. It had been due to the number of people who thronged in per day. Though the pavement had served as an extension of the restaurant, there were, still, no available seats to accommodate the overflow. The sixteen-minute drive to Bubiashie came in a flash. It turned out I had relished in his moments of engagement. With him – my first adult relationship, I had free rein to be myself. His car stereo produced some notable Ghanaian 70s funk along to which we sang. The few times our eyes met, I knew that I wanted to be with that man – in his rapture forever. We had slipped easily into a connection without the intrusion of the "will you be my girlfriend" accustomed question. After work dates transitioned to lunch pickups and drop-offs. Then there was the introduction of weekend shopping; an apparent excuse to see more of me. You see, dating in the 70s was defined by an air maturity which often swept couples into Holy matrimony without the stress as in the urban age and that's exactly what we had. My boyfriend handed me a spare key to his room at house number forty-seven on my first official visit. There - that was his proposal - the gesture which exuded his desire for exclusivity. My stomach made a light rumble, my feet got sweaty again. I knew it was how he knew best to propose but I silently wished he would say the actual words. "Do I make him work harder?" I wondered. I could not kid myself, I liked him too, No - I was in love with him. I was in love with this man, handsome and demure, who was eager to share with me his little world. A few minutes into my visit, he emerged from his chamber gussied up as if it were an occasion. With a little black box in his hand, he took my hand in his. "It's about time we journeyed to see your parents Yaa. I'm over the casualty of what we share and would want to see more of you... more permanently." Of course, it was an easy yes when he backed the delivery of the keys with a request to make us official. I was to become Mrs. Margaret Owusua Kwaakye and I could not be any more elated than that. It would have been foolish to have played the tossing game at that moment. To string along the man I had come to adore for sailing through three years of a relationship, without the incessant demand for sex would have been a swing-a-miss. With a passionate kiss, he sealed his proposal. My petite figure was buried in the frame of his masculine embrace. I stared deep into his eyes -

deep into those brown sets, like candle wax I melted in the heat of the moment. His fingers dancing passionately up and down my backless dress sent my legs into a pleasant collapse. The moan with each touch, the groan with each kiss from my neck to my chest, expressed an unspoken compatibility. "You are mine," he whispered.

Two weeks – that's how long it took for my letter to arrive in Begoro Secondary School (BEGSEC). Kissi had gained admission into BEGSEC, one of the former prides of the Eastern Region. In as much as I had a deep repugnance for accepting the obvious fact that, my little brother was the smartest of all six of us, it was so, and that had pushed him higher up the education ladder."He has an impressive command over the Queen's language. Sometimes he sounds like the white man on Ama Agyeiwaa's television box." Papa once bragged to our neighbours under the mango tree. "*Agya,* then he must work for the government or one of those gigantic white-collar corporations in the city," another chipped in. So, Kissi's admission to the secondary school created for Papa a wall of hope, a chance to relive his youthful dreams.

Hello brother,

So my letter to Kissi started,

I am writing to you today, elated. Gottfried wants to come and ask Papa for my hand in marriage. However, I worry that Mama might be unwilling to participate in the ceremony since it will be in Ankaase. I recall she had an air of discomfort when she last stopped by the village to retrieve the tiger machete she had hidden in the mukaase. Anyway, let me not soil the joyful intention behind this letter. I have sent word to Papa to have someone ready the house and prepare his ceremonial clothes.

How are you? And how is school? Hopefully, you aren't giving the teachers a run for their money with your brilliance. They call you a know-it-all, but I believe it's pure admiration of your academic excellence, coated with sheer envy. Did you receive the provisions I sent you? They were from Gottfried. I suspect that it's all a bid to be in your good books, more like to earn the support of his immediate akonta.

I am in a happy place. I can't wait to be a mother, to have my own family, a man I can call my own and the father to all my children. To have escaped the smallness of life in Ankaase was only a tiny feat compared to what I have come into. Kissi I tell you this for sure, I have struck gold with this man. I'll tell you more when we visit the village. Oh, Gottfried's mother lives in Bontriso, close to Begoro. I'll speak with him to set up an occasion for you to get acquainted. Or we could do that at my knocking ceremony, can you believe that? Knocking ceremony – your sister will soon be somebody's wife. My regards to Maa Yaa and Ayo Afumaa upon your arrival, I can't wait to see you.

Your dear sister,

Yaa Owusua.

That day was different, something out of a traditional fairy tale. My soon-to-be husband was in a pair of golden ahenema and wrapped in a green kente cloth. Maa Felicia Manku, his mother, seated at the right-hand side of the head of their delegation. She beamed with smiles revealing a wide diastema and her brown skin mingled perfectly with her cocoa print fabric. They came bearing gifts; Schnapps, several yards of cloth, tubers of yam, a white leather King James Version of the Holy Bible, and kola nuts among others which lay at the feet of Papa and our abusua panyin. Mama was present; her ebony skin glistening beneath layers of evenly spread coconut oil. She was accompanied by two of her neighbours and a relative from Jejeti.

The head of Gottfried's delegation made three sounds from his throat, loud enough to reverberate, sending all gathered into resounding silence.

"Agoo fie ha!" he greeted.

"Ameee!"

"Our people say, that when the boy brings the flower home, then it must have stood out from the weeds in the fields." He continued, "Our son, in his search for a lifelong partner, stumbled upon a lovely flower in the capital city. Well, after several enquiries, we are informed that, this flower blooms in the household of Opanyin Piesare. So we are here to do the needful to keep this flower forever."

"*Yoo, medaase*. Thank you for stating the purpose of your visit." Papa replied.

"We have seen your son," gesturing to Gottfried. "However, the Almighty had blessed my home with three daughters - all beautiful, so if your son is here, can he show us who he has been enamoured by?"

Of course, Papa and all gathered were aware that I was the reason for the occasion but somehow, this line of questioning had been mandatory in such ceremonies before my existence and it wasn't going to change with me. Ayo Afumaa and Maa Yaa were presented to the gathering, both of whom Gottfried comically rejected.

Maa Yaa, the oldest of us three, had already been married to the Amankrado of Ankaase, with whom she was expecting a child. It wasn't her first, you see, she had two children, Akosua Darkoa and Kwabena Kennedy from a previous relationship, not marriage. Afumaa on the other hand was still unmarried and with no children.

"Maggie, these people have come for your hand in marriage. They have brought your dowry and a well-declared intent to make you a part of their family. Should we accept these gifts or drive them away."

I said, pausing for dramatic effects, "*Papa mepakyew gye wai,* please accept the gifts with all gladness." Just like that, I was married. At age twenty-three I had become Mrs. Margaret Owusua Kwaakye, readied to be with the love of my life for all eternity… or so I thought. The subsequent days which followed up in my new matrimonial home came with an air of serenity in a routine, mainly marked by readying ourselves for work on weekdays - Gottfried dropping me off at my job at the Hope Paper Products and him to the GBC. The Weekends came with me rustling up varieties of delicacies for my new husband.

Kumaa had fled Ghana to Nigeria for greener pastures. I gathered it was all a ploy to join the large batch of Ghanaians marching to Germany that year. Germany, ha! Why would a son of the soil choose to shelve a life of liberty to wallow in uncertainty in the country of the round-eyed white man? I wondered. Their only desire, I had come to learn, was to cower the melanated man into slavery. But still, I was proud of her for embarking on the solo journey to financial freedom. It was the last I heard from my friend. I too pondered over what was next for me. The paper company could not be my career-defining moment. I wanted more. With my middle school qualification, I nursed new dreams - dreams of becoming a teacher.

Kojo Boadu Kwaakye was conceived three months later. A period typified by antsiness, an eagerness to witness the face of a new beginning. My husband shouldered it all; the weird late-night cravings for ice, the unreasonable bouts of tears, the brain fogs and anti-natal appointments, offering his unflinching support throughout the ten months of heaviness. Kojo Boadu's birth on that fateful Monday, 13th February 1978, opened me up to a sweet kind of pressure, the kind that comes with a worthy restlessness.

"He has your nose Yaa," Kofi said, bending over his new son at the Bubiashie Midwife's quarters. It was a rather simple space with several vivid images of childbirth on the walls. The room, accessorised by the single metallic bed with a blue leather mattress, was surprisingly well aerated to rid the fresh scent of new birth.

"Thank God we still had a bowl of your palmnut soup in the refrigerator. Had it not been Maame Pokuaa, I would have walked in here with Ga Kenkey. She told me it's advisable to serve you liquid treats for now so I jumped for whatever was left of the soup."

"You and this Pokuaa girl"

"Yaa, it's too soon. The welcoming air around this child should not be marred by bickering."

"Fine then! But you must know that I'm not pleased by your closeness to this girl. I'll ditch the topic if I do not find you two chatting in corners."

"Corners? We stood just by the entrance to our room Yaa."

"Well isn't our room at the far corner of the compound?"

"Kojo Maame, jealousy is not your best suit."

He knew better than to entertain the open invitations to flirt with this girl because, we had argued extensively about how he easily floated towards this girl the other night, even in my presence. It wasn't insecurity; it was perhaps, me fighting hard to keep my marriage intact – a little too hard, almost to the point of suffocating. Now that Kojo was here, we had a new centrepiece to our love, a new focus – him.

Chapter 4
The huge debacle

"When the clouds are full, they'll empty themselves," was the conclusive line in the letter I wrote to Kissi. After spending his last long vacation with us, he had become privy to the innermost happenings of my home. Ours was a thin-walled chamber-and-hall self-contained after all.

"When the clouds are full, they'll empty themselves," I once heard my father murmur to himself on a cold night, a coldness not of the weather but one of Mama's heated tantrums. He told me, that it was from that night that he knew that Mama had one foot out of their union. 1979, the year things went haywire. My husband resigned from his job at the GBC to invest his savings and a bit of mine into a start-up. It was the year the Jerry John Rawlings' military regime overthrew the Supreme Military Council but somehow, Kofi found means to kick start and keep a business afloat in the tumult. It was the year of the uprising in Ghana, which resulted from perceived bad governance and corruption, yet in the chaos, we surprisingly thrived. My husband bought and sold goods of all kinds, all sophisticated office and household wares. With a portion of the liquid capital, he rented out a space at Kaneshie, not too far from where we lived at Bubiashie house number forty-seven. The amiable man drew in

people from all walks of life to his trade. The powerful connections he had made during his time at the GBC were highly beneficial to the new venture. They thronged **Gottfried and sons** to pawn their television sets, ghetto blasters, washing machines etc or to simply trade them for new and modern ones. He would then sell the old ones to some Middle Easterners who shipped these used goods overseas for reasons known only to them. My husband, whose interest was in the cedis, knew better than to probe these Middle Easterners further. He came up with that easy name, Gottfried and Sons for reasons I found amusing.

"*Odo* I'm sure you could come up with a better name. Come on put your brain to test."

"My brain is convinced that this name is good. It would lure in customers."

"Lure in? Try repelling." I laughed for a long time.

"It lacks originality, something typical of petty trades started by uneducated folks who have come into new money."

"And so is your ***Here At Last Tradings***. It oozes struggles."

"No, it breathes the period of relief after a struggle. And which other son do you have to attach ***and sons*** to your business?"

"Kojo Boadu is the first of many to come. The First of the five sons you'll soon bear."

I laughed harder till tears clouded my vision. "You're not serious," I said, shoving his elevated frame out of my way to attend to little Kojo on the potty in the bathroom. Though I loved the idea of having more children, I wanted us to plan carefully towards ushering them into the world. They must live a good life than we did growing up, I thought.

Among his many connections was Mr. Damptey Kyem, the owner of the popular Damptey Kyem printing press where Kissi worked on vacations, a kind courtesy to my husband. He had put in a word for my brother when he expressed interest in earning an income on school breaks. "Sister, can you please ask Mr. Kofi if he could help me get a job or, make me his assistant at the shop?" Mr. Kofi - it was how he addressed my husband. I brought it to my husband's ear, and less than forty-eight hours after a meeting with Mr. Damptey Kyem, Kissi was hired as a floor assistant at the printing press. They operated in the manner of Hope Paper Products.

The money was good. Life was comfortable. Yet I could not bring myself to understand how a business, barely a year old, was already making thousands of cedis that fast. It wasn't too long after when we made our first five million cedis. With every weekend came new faces - very unfamiliar faces. The way my husband proudly called them friends dizzied me. None of them were dignified in my opinion, all of them loud and boorish. I engaged in talks bigger than their lives; on money, politics, plans to acquire lands and hushed talks I perceived were about women. In between bites they made snarky remarks about unwitting co-tenants who walked past the gathering to do one thing or the other. I wondered how Kofi had come by the,m to begin with. He revealed too much about us and the business, making them all interested in selling one thing or the other to him in exchange for double the money they had spent to acquire it.

Since my brother had a vacation job, and did not have to stay back in Begoro with my in-laws to assist them on the farm on breaks from Wenchi Secondary School, He stayed with us to commute to Damptey Kyem also in Bubiashie. This was the final Form-five vacation, where many students prepared towards enrollment in other schools for their Sixth-form education - which heralded their entry to tertiary institutions. He had been accepted to the Presbyterian Boys Secondary School, Legon in Accra. I remember he would say, whenever I dared to cajole him to opt for another school, perhaps St. Augustine's or Adisadel College in the Cape Coast, "Sister, don't you know that there are only two schools? It's PRESEC and the rest o." There was no stopping him; whatever he put his mind to, he did. A trait I had come to despise and admire at the same time. He only did two years at Begoro Secondary School and continued to Wenchi Secondary School for the third to fifth year because, his sponsor, my elder brother Yaw Asare, had come out of Training College and could no longer afford his fees at BEGSEC. The tuition at the Secondary School at

Wenchi was free because Yaw had been employed there as a teacher.

Kissi had noticed the excesses in our decoration. The new sofas with velvet covers, the Toyota Corolla sedan parked on the compound, the gigantic desktop computer on the corner table - an air of coming into new money. I waited to hear his comments, some questions even, to be thrown at me for answers. I needed to say something to someone. We were by ourselves, my husband stood outside the gate with baby Kojo and two of his many new friends. But Kissi said nothing. I sat back on the sofa, assailed. "When do you go to school?" I asked dutifully. I thought it wise to reassume my place as a big sister at that moment, to bring some lightness to the atmosphere. My chest heavy with unspoken lamentations, I kept the conversation going, saving it all up for my next letter to my brother. We gave it a name, *"The Bulletin."*

Hello brother,

Many questions consume my thoughts as I write to you. But first, how are you? And how is the new school treating you?

I paid a visit to Ankaase a week after your departure. You know Papa has yet to see Kojo Boadu since the naming ceremony. They've grown an attachment to these two. Anyway, I'm sure you took notice of the changes in my home on your last visit. The matter is that Mr. Kofi has come about some wealth that I don't understand. I know, you think I'm beginning to sound like the pessimistic wife with a sickening fear of success. But this one is worrying. I fear he may be exposing himself and even our family to danger. Don't let me get started on the people he calls friends. He's never been the type to frolic with the uncouth. I'm sure he's engaging in dubious deals. He's suddenly become a nightlife connoisseur.

Nana Dwomor, our taxi driver neighbour, had informed me about a scene at the shop. Kofi had been harassed by some thugs who speculated that my husband sold them many stolen goods. Brother and the sad part? He did not trust me enough to tell me till after I confronted him about it. With wealth comes corruption, especially when it comes this fast and easy. I miss the days he used to work at GBC. Those were simpler days. If this new persona of his does not stop, I foresee a lot of embarrassment in our future. At this point what I feel goes beyond exhaustion.

It's true what they say that, when the clouds are full they'll empty themselves. I can no longer keep silent on his misbehaviour and huge debacles in our future and I do not want to stay till then.

Write to me soon.

Your dear sister,

Yaa Owusua.

Ghanaian Men, well most of them, continue to find it difficult to heed the counsel of their wives. I was hitched to one. It was the Christmas of 1981, a year after my brother had returned from his service with the American Field Service (AFS) in Switzerland. It was about six days before the second coup d'état in the country. Some people said they saw it coming, others like myself, well, not so much. They said it appeared like the Hilla Limann-led People's National Party (PNP), ruled beneath the shadows of the Armed Forces Revolutionary Council (AFRC) which metamorphosed into the Provisional National Defence Council (PNDC). Perhaps I was too Self-involved and family-inclined to nurture an interest in politics. It was a "Holy War," as said by Rawlings, waged against the PNP for the disappointment to offer effectual leadership.

My brother became the first of the Asare bunch to ever travel on the white man's aeroplane to the white man's land. In Switzerland, he stayed with a white family, something our father became overly proud of. After enrolling successfully at PRESEC, he became what he called an "AFSer," after volunteering with the organisation on campus. There, an opportunity sprung forth to join other volunteers on a one-year exchange program in September of 1979 and were to return in September of 1980. My son had turned three and my husband, well, still the same. Except for this time, there were upheavals; our finances had taken a downturn, and we could no longer easily afford a proper Sunday home-cooked meal; his favourite fufu with loaded meat soup. Accusations of selling stolen goods came running through our doors. Every day was another story. It was humiliating to see that the once revered couple had become a topic in rumours and anecdotes. Life had dwindled to a place of ridicule within three years.

"I want out of this marriage Kofi." The Words slipped out surprisingly with ease at the table. "I've had enough of everything; the shame is too much to bear."

Silence covered the atmosphere for half an hour. Kofi said nothing, occasionally looking up from his bowl of food. I didn't even bring up the many times he cheated on me in times of abundance. How did I know? He confessed. At the many times my *find a cheater radar* went off, he got caught. That in addition to his pig pigheadedness flushed the business down the drain, was reason enough.

"Yaa, I've changed," he said, breaking the stiffening silence. "You've done well to have stood by me through the many debacles. All the times I was apprehended by the police, you were there. I was innocent and it…"

"Innocent? Once or even twice is pardonable but when it begins to settle into normalcy then measures must be put in place."

Truth was I worried for my son and what he might replicate from his father. I loved him, I truly did. But sometimes, love just isn't enough to hold on to. A month later, soon after my family returned the customary Schnapps to his family, I moved into a vacant room at my old residence – to house number forty-five, as a single mother.

Chapter 5
Fresh starts and abrupt end in Lagos

Lagos was disorienting; All 1,171 km^2 of it. I stood like a needle in a haystack, completely buried beneath the many people who marched to and fro the bus station; some aimlessly, others off-loading goods from remote places from the carriage of rickety buses. Luggage moved all over, notable of them the blue and red checked bags, which would later become an emotional symbol in the history of Ghanaians in Nigeria. The bags mostly landed on the heads of some visibly strong young men and women; they called them *'alagbaru,'* who readily assisted commuters from one point to the other at a fee. The conductors of the yellow Volkswagen 33 *Danfo* buses, clamoured for the attention of prospective passengers with their noisy hailing.

A sweltering heat blanketed the atmosphere – drying up my lips in an instant. "I have to find Nkechi," I thought, staring at the black-and-white photograph in my hand. Almost impossible to tell whether this lady was truly as light as the sun like Dauda had included in his many descriptions of her. He had sent word to the lady to guide me through Lagos. Keeping my composure in those lengthy conversations with Dauda took a lot of practice. He did not enunciate the 'h' in heat, hug, how, or high he left out the 'h' in every word. *Chop* sounded like *shop* and it became difficult to hold my laughter. On quiet days, I would recall examples and just burst into laughter.

"Maggie, teachers day for igh demand for Naija na. Na dem dey get work wey dey pay better moni. Una for leave ere go try luck for di-er," was what he said one time. Dauda had left Northern Nigeria to Lagos, then to Accra for trade. He took up a Ghanaian Fante woman and found himself at home in the Motherland. Before I departed from Accra, Dauda had joined the Bubiashie church of Pentecost where his wife worshipped.

If you would recall, I had left the hinterlands for the city as a Junior Secondary School graduate with no formal training in any endeavour. But Dauda made that happen. Without having to sit in a classroom, He got me a certificate, qualifying me as a teacher. It looked no different from the authentic certificate of his wife, Eduafoa. "Baba Dee," that's how I fondly addressed him. "You be sharp pass! How you fit pull this one off na?" I asked in more refined pidgin. I trusted him to show that grin, the one he displayed whenever I tried overly hard to identify with him. But Dauda would further engage me as a gesture of appreciation. Perhaps, it was how the Queen's language rolled off my tongue with a self-taught American accent. Mainly characterised by an exaggerated 'r' sound in each word, that impressed

Dauda as it did with others – predominantly the middle and lower classes.

Leaving my son behind was the toughest decision of my adult life. At only age four, he had to be separated from me and placed in the care of his father, my ex-husband. The pursuit of financial stability took a terrible toll on my personal life. Waking up that fateful Friday, the 19th of February 1982, with my bags packed from the night before, I dropped my son off with Kofi at his residence. He posed a series of questions, unveiling a measure of hidden concerns. But he looked pale – a complete shadow of his former self. With a kiss on his cheek, I placed my sleeping toddler on the cushioned chair and made my way to the Accra-Tema bus station yard. There, I joined the many ambitious Ghanaians who sought a fresh chapter.

From the Aflao-Togo border, through the Togo-Cotonou border, to the Cotonou-Lagos border, I had a rude awakening. In the tribulations with Kofi, I left my marriage and now my son, in search of greener pastures. "Had I become my mother?" Papa had once said that Mama 'chased' money now. An act I had strongly condemned, yet here I was reliving the ugly truth from the past. But it wasn't my fault entirely right? It was Kofi's. Had he heeded my counsel and my occasional nags, our financial scuffles could have been prevented. Again – this was how Mama had lamented during Papa's crisis. I had indeed become my mother. I prayed silently with a heavy heart, "Help me, Lord."

Once we cleared the Badagry border onto the dual carriage Lagos road, I knew I was someplace far from home. Much of that area still looked like a construction site. Foreign companies, I would later come to know, were behind the busy erections and had plans to raise more skyscrapers across the city of Lagos. In this new oil-fired economy of Nigeria, every dream, I came to believe, was possible.

Nkechi was light-skinned, light like the sun as Baba Dee had described. From the station at Amuwo-Festac town, we jumped into another bus bound for Ebutte Metta plying the Lagos-Badagry expressway. Ebutte Metta looked close to home - like an old town. The dusty inner roads, some dilapidated houses and roadside food vendors mimicked Bubiashie. "You sabi di school wey you dey go teach?" Nkechi asked on arrival at the house Dauda had previously arranged for a comfortable stay in Lagos. "No oo, he talk me say ein friend go come in two days to sort that out for me." She nearly broke into a laugh. Seeing how I struggled to speak like her.

"Dat one too dey o. but errm teacher Maggie, if you see am wey you no gree teach, dem open some kind private school for Aloba street. That one good sha! My friend talk say dem dey find new teachers."

"Ah Nkechi, you dey too good! Thank you."

"Relax omo-Ghana, you don't have to try hard with me. I guess I should have started with a simpler tongue."

"You didn't have to put me through all that ahh!"

We shared a familiar laugh, as though we had known each other for a long time. I wondered why we barely interacted on the fifty-four-minute drive from Amuwo. It would have been a shorter duration if the driver had not stopped for passengers or to hurl friendly insults at fellow drivers. The room was small - smaller than I was used to. At a glance, one would deem it as though it may be poorly aerated but the iron rod-barricaded windows allowed in some fresh air from the trees in the backyard. On the cemented floor lay a medium-density double mattress, a wooden rocking chair in the corner and a study table beneath which a stainless steel bucket stood. "This would do," I thought silently.

Ehiziojie lived next door. He was a part-time truck driver who at other times played the role of a site worker on one of the many construction sites. Nkechi had first walked me to his door for an introduction. For a man living in such quarters, he was well kept with a beautiful set of teeth well-pedicured feet clad in bluebird flip flops, a decent Yoruba man by all standards.

Salvation Cluster of Schools stood adjacent to the highway. It stood next to a Secondary School under construction. A week after I arrived in the Fatherland, Nkechi arranged a meeting with the principal of the school at his Abule Nla Road residence. Ei but why are most of these Nigerian men light-skinned? I wondered. A closer look at his knuckles and grasped that his complexion originated from over the counter. The Principal - Akin Adeyemi, the would-have-been dark-skinned man, was about 5 feet 6 inches tall. He smiled boldly. Every sentence and question began and ended with '*eeh.*' He was a heavy man whose cheeks wobbled with every laugh with deep fine lines, giving him away in age. After emptying a bottle of Guinness within a rather short conversation, he had agreed without demanding my certificate, to have me teach the English language to the Junior Secondary School students. "*eeh* Maggie, the way you speak this your English, one would assume you had stayed in the Americas or Britain other than Ghana *eeh.*"

Flatteries! Perhaps I had over-wooed Akin with my American twang. Every distinct word came with echoes or rolling 'Rs.' "Maggie was a highly respected teacher in Ghana. You see, their government isn't being financially fair to the teachers." I wasn't in the place to discuss Rawlings' Military junta in my new happy place.

"Na work I come dey find o, we shouldn't talk politics tonight."

"There she goes with her oyibo-infused pidgin," Nkechi added.

The school was welcoming. By April of 1982, I had settled into my role as an English language tutor.

The favour of God was heavily working for my good, but at the time, my thinking centred on vanity. It attributed the many opportunities to my beauty. I did get carried away by the many compliments my petite physique and shiny brown skin reeled in. My many admirers found me a rarity – well spoken, beautiful and independent Ghanaian woman. It got into my head.

"*Omo Ghana,* you too fine ah ah!" were among the many praises heaped on me on the streets. Omo Ghana was an ethnic slur for Ghanaians. We had one for them too, it was *alatafuo* or *anago*. As long as both countries kept the mutual respect going, no offence was taken.

Ehiziojie dropped me off at school in the truck. Had I declined his offer that time, I'm sure he would have pegged me as an uppity neighbour. I had politely waved him off many times but this time the relentless gentleman had added a honk, drawing attention from other commuters. What was all that for? I pondered. He had been keen on fetching me into his truck but this – was a cheap stunt. However, I caved because I saw no other way out of the piercing eyes of the on-lookers.

"Let this be the last time you'll engage me in such a play." I finally said after arriving at the school's premises.

"No vex now. It was the only way to get your attention."

"Well, that was quite shallow. You are lucky I'm such a lady if not, you would have been a morning dose of undiluted insults and side-eyes."

He laughed, his eyes staring deep into mine. It was the way he threw his confidence in my face. I didn't hate it – I had found it admirable.

"Then help me do better. It's no mystery that I feel something deep for you but this kind hide and seek play wey you dey play ah ah!"

"Try harder Ehiz. No, do better. Try discarding these cheap stunts. Public spectacles aren't my thing you know."

"*Omo Ghana* with standards! Pardon my naivety. Make *una* no vex. Do you mind if I pick you up from work?"

"*Heiii*!" I roared with laughter. "Is it your master's truck that you want to turn into a private service? Please don't get yourself fired for my sake. I may not be able to cope with that."

That man Ehiz! His intentions were clear as day. He wanted more than just to be neighbours. Was I in the mental space to entertain another man? No. Did I enjoy the attention derived from eligible bachelors? Yes. But you see, the truth is, I was still in recovery from my failed marriage. The ride to work was unnecessary. For a kobo or two, I could engage the service of an okada rider to the school. There were times when the parents of some of my students offered rides halfway to school. On other days I was in the red, I marched the entire fifteen to twenty minutes to the premises, which in this case I would have preferred to Ehiz's truck.

I earned a decent income. Decent enough to splurge on wax prints at the textile aisle at the Ikeja market. On okada rides to oyingbo bus station, Mushin, we joined the mid-morning voyagers on the *danfo* to Ikeja. Shola, my new acquaintance resided two blocks away from my residence. She, in the company of Nkechi and her Ghanaian boyfriend, Berima led the way to the stalls of Busola, a middle-aged overweight woman. Busola would later come to play a pivotal role in my safe return to Ghana when Shehu Shagari, the then Nigerian President, reiterated the words which led to the expulsion of millions of immigrants, the majority of whom were Ghanaians.

Some locals blamed us for 'taking all' their jobs. They blamed non-Nigerians for their joblessness. Soft chaos swept the streets and the corridors of my mind. Fate played unfairly against me, I thought. In the face of a global economic slowdown, the Nigerian oil-fired economy began to waver. There was a scuffle for jobs. Even the educated middle class competed with the lower class for menial jobs. In silence, I prayed that my false documents would not be made. Every day outside my home was every day in panic. It was reported that a handful of unruly locals had attacked a mélange of immigrants including Ghanaians. Some were beaten badly, others were forced to flee the area – an act later condemned by the local authorities. "Why now?" I asked staring at the skies as though, expecting an answer to fall on my face.

"They should all be arrested, tried and made to return to their homes. Illegal immigrants should not be given any notice whatsoever. If you break a law, then you have to pay for it." said Shehu Shagari, the Nigerian President who favoured long hats. Echoes of the powerful sing-song voice stuck with me on that fateful morning of January 17th 1983. I panicked.

President Shagari's campaign had sought to reclaim the Nigerian land from the influx of 'Aliens' in a worsening economy. We were given till the 31st of January to exit the Fatherland. Nkechi and Shola were supportive. They helped me lay low till I had readied myself to depart for Ghana. It was wise to limit the number of times I took unnecessary after-dinner strolls. Teaching however continued till we were relieved of duty in about April of 1983. I stuck to the same old habitual tasks as though I was unperturbed. At least not until a failed attempt at robbery blighted what was left of a long day.

Chapter 6

Ghana must Go

The Rawlings administration blocked the Ghana-Togo border, making it impossible for citizens fleeing Nigeria at President Shagari's command to return home. Many of whom, unlike me, who had no desire to 'wait and see' what happens next, crammed all they could in the checked tote bag, which then became a defining symbol of expulsion, "Ghana must go."

Those who already made it to Benin became refugees, waiting positively for news regarding the reopening of the border. Those relied highly on external aids to survive. That statistics, I was unwilling to be a part of. So, I switched to tying scarves with every outfit, ending all sentences with *'naw'* or *'ahn ahn,'* speaking pidgin English with a forceful accent, and screaming a sharp *"eeeeehhn?"* to petrifying tales - quintessentially Nigerian.

Journeying home from Femi's house was always a hectic one. But that day was good because I had been paid. He lived on Jebba Street, the plush side of Ebutte Metta. I wondered why his parents did not enrol him and his brothers in one of the many fancy schools with ridiculous names in Lagos. The Ajayis were filthy rich, wealthy enough to even purchase the entire Salvation School. They were rumoured to own the land on which the school was erected. I was hired by Mr Ajayi as a private tutor for Femi. After a PTA meeting, he approached me for comments on Femi's performance. Upon revelations of his son's poor academics, especially in English composition and comprehension, I was hired immediately.

"You must to teach my son well well till he begin dey speak like you." He remarked. Mr. Ajayi had not had the luxury of education. He had come into money by buying and selling anything he laid his hands on. Later in life, he veered into construction and immersed himself in the oil sector. That man knew people in high places. He was friends with top politicians and I even heard that he had a personal relationship with Shehu Shagari. He hardly spoke in public. When he did, people silently mocked him, he knew that. One would understand why he wanted different for Femi.

It was between 9 – 10 pm when I arrived at my gate. It was locked. Our street was dark, lonely and highly unsafe for a woman. No one came to my aid after kicking and banging on the gate for half an hour.

"*Omo Ghana*, wetin you dey do for here?" said a thick tall man on an okada. His face was partially concealed beneath a large cap. Behind him sat a light-skinned man who grinned weirdly at me.

"*Oya* bring your bag. Do am easy. Make we no wound una for here." he added. It was a prolonged struggle for my purse. The skinny man and I posed at the gate as though we were in a game of tug-of-war, only to stumble and fall with a thud on my side. A single heave by the muscular man had sent me into a crumble. The skinny man moved his right hand menacingly on his hips, visibly angered by my audacity to resist his attack; He pulled out a kitchen fork from his back pocket.

"Ah ah ajei ajei ahh help help! Please stop." I cried.

I bled profusely from the deep multiple stab wounds on my right breast, torso, thigh and legs.

"*Ewu* ooo! Thief! Thief! Come and help o, they want to kill somebody o." screamed a woman. The gate finally came unlocked and the two men sped off on the okada. In a prone position, I made my way through the gates into the compound. I saw the face of the woman who called out to save my life. It was the obese, middle-aged wax print dealer from Ikeja, Busola. There was no time to query her presence in my neighbourhood. There was a gathering of scents. My landlord's wife brought out some pills, ground them into powder and poured them on my leg and thigh wounds.

"Make una comot her dress and put some of the powder on the chest one." Said a co-tenant, Amara.

"People dey here now, make I carry am go inside so that you and Chinyere can do that," Ehiz added. Chinyere was the landlord's wife.

I slipped into sweet unconsciousness as Ehiz scooped me into his arms. It felt as though, I was falling. Am I dying? I caught myself asking as it all went dark.

"Take dis one. *E-go* suit you well well." Busola said, handing me a bundle of wax print. She was right it was a fine print. Streaks of gold on a brown print favoured my skin.

"Okay give me twelve yards of this one and six yards of the blue with the abstract design," I said.

"*heeiiii*!! Abstract *ke*?" she said clapping her chubby hands and resting them on her wide hips. "Nkechi, you did not tell me you were coming to my shop with Queen Elizabeth today. Okay Ma, no problem." We all burst into laughter in unison, as though it was rehearsed.

"Mama please forget my grammar and add the green one on the top shelf."

"That one na Holland o. That one too cost sha."

"Am I complaining?" the loud cheers from my friends which followed, drew unnecessary attention to the stall of the fabric queen of the market square. The radio box at the market came cheap. So together with that, I purchased two music cassette tapes. I thought it was about time I livened up my space. I loved music. It was to me as therapy. When muscles ached and limbs were sore, music would whisk me into a comfort zone. With many tingles penetrating my body, my stiffened muscles always heaved with relief when music came on the radio box. When words failed, the music told me what I couldn't express.

'Lady' by the incomparable Fela Kuti and Africa 70 was one of my many favourites at the time.

'If you call a woman

African woman, no go gree

She goes say, she goes say, I be lady, oh

If you call a woman

African woman, no go 'gree

She go say (she go say, I be lady, oh)

She go say market woman na woman

She go say, she go say I be lady oh.'

When his songs came on, I looked forward to the extended play of instrumentals before the smooth introduction of his rich manly voice. His saxophone seeped into a sea of other instruments creating a danceable and pleasant sound to the ear. That could only be brewed by Fela Kuti, one of the greatest to ever do it. The evening playlists were romance-themed, mainly fuelled by sounds from Dolly Parton.

'Yesterday is gone, gone

But tomorrow is forever

No more crying, tears leave tracks

And memories find their way back

Tomorrow's waiting

let's journey there together.'

With Dolly's words, I slipped into the free world of imagination, where I chased the sunset with my Prince charming at the seashore. At this point, I do know what you're thinking, that I was so much of a hopeless romantic for a woman with a failed marriage. And that's right! This was so because I had experienced what love was not hence I craved for what it was. It was how I lived the remaining months in Ebutte Metta till the robbery which had me hospitalised for two weeks and placed on sick leave for a month. The trauma from the attack was not one to easily get over or sweep under the carpet as though it had not occurred. Life was hard. Socializing after school became impossible for me. Whenever the sun took away its lights, paving the way for the moon to show up, I'd have panic attacks. Its sight reminded me of how it had failed to come to my aid when I lay in a pool of my own blood.

Busola, sent over many clothes and soups through Barima and Shola when they came to visit. Soon, my room was filled with piles of fabrics, yam, fruits, soup bowls, assorted vegetables, meat and confectioneries. Ehiz and Chinyere came over with some money. Ehiz did so weekly till I resumed teaching. Some of my students even offered to fill my drums with water from the community tap. Mr. Ajayi came by with the School's principal one evening with a fat envelope. Unbelievable! He also mentioned how Femi had missed my presence in their home and how he felt partly responsible for the occurrence. The outpour of love was overwhelming, and my fears quickly idled in its presence. Perfect love casts away all fear indeed. Whatever perception I had held regarding Nigerians faded away. The respect I had garnered in that community was unknown to me until the mishap. It's true what they say about living life well, you never know who is watching. When news came out that Rawlings had reopened the border in October of 1983, I knew it was time to return home - return to Ghana at least until the immigration tumult died down.

"My daughter, Tawfiq will take you to the bus station. My husband's bus leaves for Ghana tonight and he go make sure say you go arrive safely." With this Busola handed me a bag, in it were many bundles of cloths again, dried fish and meat, yellow gari and some money. "You fit change the money when you arrive in Ghana." dumbfounded, I hugged her tightly and whispered many lines of God bless you. Side-by-side, Nkechi sat with me as we journeyed to the bus station.

"You know I will be back when it's calm right?"

"You had better!"

"Thank you Nkechi, I'll send word when I arrive safely in Accra."

Again, I joined the many Ghanaians who sat in silence on the voyage home.

Chapter 7

New goals & the 1983 drought

The drought in Ghana resulting from the insurrection of the Rawlings Military regime deepened in 1983. I see that the economic and environmental blunders from the time still carry on into the present date. My country learnt nothing. With no laudable solutions on the table, we continued to wallow in the chaos with prayers that "this too shall pass." I returned to an empty and hungry country. Thank God for Busola's goodies. They sustained me for a while but it was not long till I joined the many who queued for uncooked kenkey. Its uncooked form was called *'aflata'* which directly translates to *complete mix.* That food made from fermented corn dough became a hot commodity in the country. We queued with stones, sticks, chairs and even buckets in our stead overnight for some balls of the *aflata.* All these, by products of the rampant bushfires which destroyed major farmlands, markets and properties coupled with the governmental upheavals transformed Ghana into something I did not recognise. The country was tumultuous. But home remained home. The country side though experiencing its fair share of the drought was far better than the city. Life was slightly calm and uncomplicated.

Christmas in 1983 remained dry in the city. Though food was not in excess the village still had enough to go around its people. Ankaase looked mystical at that time of the year. Early mornings in December draped in thick fog, completely concealing the mountains encamping the village. The afternoon air ushered in the scent of greens from the forest which hemmed Ankaase – a scent I had come to appreciate after being away for so long. Harmattan reared its dry head a lot in the afternoons. It was the perfect air of Christmas. It is to us what snow is to white men in the festive season. The moonlights themed the night for *Anansesem* by the fireside under the mango tree, or on the compound of a village elder who volunteered to steer the night. We listened to stories and lore told of the great goddess of the Birim River and her marriage to the god of the Pra River, the adventures of *Ananse* the spider and why the crab had no head.

Maa Yaa, the oldest female of my siblings mostly coordinated these gatherings during the festive season. We cooked and shared meals, exchanged gifts and filled one another in on the has-beens of life. Children went from house to house for candies and goodies. *"Afe hyia pa o,"* they greeted, *"Afe nko mme to yɛn"* we'd respond. With this, we poured candies into their bowls or offered some money in the absence of it.

Mama still lived at Jejeti. She did not join the rest of us to mark the end of the year. I was informed of a little drama which had come about in my absence. It was a scuffle between Mama and her younger sister. Yes, Mama had a sister, one with whom she hadn't been on great terms for years. They argued over farmlands left to them by their father, Opanyin Nyarko. Mama being the older of the two was put in charge of the inheritance. Her sister, Oforiwaa was not the type to succumb to authority. When she received word in the Western Region that Mama had returned to Jejeti, she immediately packed her bags to sojourn to their parental home. Though there was an appearance of sisterliness in the public's eye, pressure brewed beneath the surface between the two. A week after Oforiwaa arrived in the town, Mama fled Jejeti to Asante Asaman, where her parents originally hailed. There too, she had acres of land she was in charge of. Her sister in the knowledge of this, travelled to Asaman a year later, perhaps to keep an eye on Mama to ensure she had nothing sinister up her sleeves. Oforiwaa's presence awoke internal strife - power struggles between the two made the family home inhospitable. Frimpong, a paternal cousin, narrated the many times the two sisters called for unwanted attention with their open squabbles. Mama, growing fed up with the debacles, fled Asante Asaman again to Jejeti.

Akosua Darkoa, the first of Maa Yaa's daughters and the second of her six children was all grown. Our closeness in age had established for us a good rapport. Her mother had her and Kennedy earlier than the remaining four - three of whom belonged to the Amankrado and the other, Akua Denkyira from a relationship prior with the Amankrado. She was an ambitious soul that Darkoa. She wanted to do and become many things and dreamt of seeing the rest of the world outside of Ankaase. Unlike her other siblings, we had a stronger connection and flowed towards each other when in the same space. She was going to be a big star…that one. Again, I would sojourn to Nigeria with her in hopes of escaping the shores of Africa. At the family gathering that year, Maa Yaa thought it wise to have Akos move in with me at Bubiashie. In her words, 'whose footsteps were worthy of emulation than Yaa Maggie's,' She thought with Akos' determination to win at life, It was best to have her sit at my feet. I wouldn't have had it any other way.

With the biggest smile of approval I answered, "Oh why not?" supporting my family by any means necessary was what I lived for but this to me, was my shot at inserting myself in a sisterhood… when it came to my family, I was a people pleaser which with truth, was simply a trait of fear - a fear of being cast out.

Our farmlands served us well into the New Year. The earth brought forth her bud to cater for our household. The river, though reduced in volume, gave out the best of fishes. Kojo Boadu, my five-year-old son, was Papa's little aide. Those two were inseparable. Papa's lap was to Kojo for sleeping, eating and so on. With each stare came a gleam of pride. It was to say, "Maggie you have done a good thing." Papa had come to be a man of few words, so his eyes communicated his thoughts.

Kissi looked better than when I last saw him. Switzerland had left him an air of sophistication. When alone, we told each other stories of what had been. I shared with him the great tragedy in Lagos.

"We should be thankful you weren't killed. I can never fathom why you thought it a great idea to start over by yourself in Nigeria."

"But I'm here no,w, aren't I? Sometimes man must do what's necessary to survive. It will be a shame to sit by and watch life pass me by."

"Speaking of life, what's the way forward? What do you intend to do back home sister?"

"*Hmm,* I don't know but I'm considering venturing into trading second-hand clothes."

"Second-hand clothes?"

"*Hmm aane* o, I'm informed on how lucrative it is. I know of a woman who has built a three-bedroom house from this business and I too would like to build my own house someday and possibly expand to other market centres outside Kantamanto."

"Well, it's good to know you have a plan."

"However unfortunate I was in Nigeria will not deter me from my goals. You know Maggie is an unstoppable force." We laughed for a while after this. Kissi pledged to support me on this venture with all he had saved from his trip to Switzerland. The organisation which sponsored their trip was generous to have provided them with some pocket money. Some of which he had saved and kept with Yaw Asare in Wenchi. It amounted to four hundred dollars which was pegged for about 24,000 cedis on the black market at the time. Kissi had given me the boost of a lifetime.

With the help of a few good women at the market square, I made necessary contacts with the authorities in charge of allocating sheds at the second-hand clothing hub to lease out a plot for my sales. 1984 came in with calm, incomparable to that which I've ever felt. Every step I took aligned with my goal of being better than I was years before - financially and physically. To think that I didn't have to pay Kissi back for the money given me made me smile more. "I'm on track," I said to myself many times. Indeed I was, heading in the right direction towards making it big and thank God I had a brother to believe in my dreams, however ambitious they were.

In his final year at the University of Ghana, I made several visits to my brother and he returned it. He was the smartest of my father's children, so it didn't come as a surprise when he read a double major in Spanish and Economics. Bowls of soups and stews from my kitchen did not pass him by. Kissi enjoyed my cooking and so did his room 515 mates. It was the era of black and white photography where all pictures appeared as a dull grey version of reality. So, with a camera he had purchased on his trip to Switzerland, Kissi started a private photography business. His was a coloured film camera - one of the very few in the country at the time. After taking some random shots, he would air-mail the films to Switzerland for them to be developed. Later, it would become a lucrative pastime for Kissi, setting him up for an ambitious future.

"Sister, say 'cheeeeese'," he shouted from the second floor of Legon Hall Annex B one Saturday evening. I held on tightly to my food basket, looked up and flashed a smile. That frozen second would later become my favourite photo and memory of my brother.

Kantamanto was hot. Its traders were vicious. There, my diplomacy stood no chance. If you wanted to feed your family or break even at the close of business day, you had to wrap your waist in savagery and your head with the skill of coercion - these together with assertiveness came in handy to survive as a trader in the square.

In a single stretch sheltering women from all backgrounds, we sold similar products and called out to passers-by almost in unison to patronise our goods. We even went as far as grabbing and dragging them to our sheds and it worked. They always ended up with a single pillowcase or bed sheet to placate us.

The men often stopped by my shed. In their bid to woo me, they would buy multiple items and spend endless minutes engaging me in meaningless conversations. I noticed the side-eyes from my competitors. I did not care; instead, I took full advantage of whatever attracted them to me. It appeared they were obsessed with the fullness of my lips and how I kept them coated in lipsticks. So I purchased a bunch of them in crimson and café to highlight their thickness, I threw in a new bottle of 'Lady Lady Brown powder to enhance my already chocolate skin. Now all I had to do was flash a smile a say *"Hello my dear, to bi ma mi wai odo,"* like a charm, they gravitated towards my shed to purchase whatever I had for sale. Business was good and soon I was selling out three to four bales of second-hand goods in two to three weeks.

Akua Denkyira - the third of Maa Yaa's children - Joined me in the trade. She left Ankaase to join me in the capital. The word industrious did not do her justice. Akua worked hard. Whatever her hand touched she sold with ease. There was something to be said about her commitment to the work; it made her endearing. But as you know, a woman with little education at the time and even in this day and age would embrace a call to marriage speedily. It was a comfortable choice away from education.

Marriage – it was what labeled our existence as women in my day. Dr. Kwegyir Aggrey's big quote about female education held water, but to the high and slightly above average earning families at the time. Today, it's refreshing to see women take up roles and offices which were otherwise thought for men. Later, Akua would, without much contemplation, settle with her teacher-lover in Tekyiman.

Chapter 8

My greatest love & Mama's betrayal

The rush for *Aburokyire* was on. Everyone sought ways to flee the hardships of the Ghanaian economy for well-paying menial jobs overseas, particularly in Germany. The European Nation had become appealing to my generation especially the restless returnees from Nigeria who sought means to redeem their image. Akosua Darkoa's visit to my residence had me running back to Dauda to help me travel again to Nigeria, this time, with my niece.

Word went around that it was easier to enter Germany through Lagos. This was so because Nigerians had some kind of good standing with Germans hence, most applicants in the West-African country were granted visas from the consulate easily. And indeed it was so. Also, at the time, documentation was easily forged; if two files were placed before you, it was impossible to tell which was counterfeit. Nigerians did it well, a more reason I enjoyed being in their company, they'll get the job done and tell no one. The weekend leading to the journey was chaotic and stressful. Buying this, packing that and to be honest, the sudden call for change disconcerted me. I worried about the atmosphere in Lagos and the shock from the attack during the expulsion of immigrants. It had been seven years, but the trauma lingered. Returning to this country in a bid to get Akosua out of the continent left me with questions about my safety. Also, since my relationship with Kwame Ayew had hit the rocks, I thought it was best to give myself a break.

Kwame Ayew - the love of my life - the man in whose presence I melted. That man loved me and I did too. We met on the Easter of 1986. He had returned from France for vacation and was out with his group of well-dressed and good-looking men around North Kaneshie, enjoying the merriness of the season. From the first "hello" we hit it off. It felt familiar; his presence, the conversation, the walk to the taxi and the "see you soon." So when he jokingly said, "I think we were cats together in our previous lives," I knew he felt it too. He picked me up the next weekend for a time out with his colleagues at the Restaurant by the Dansoman beach. Clinton, one of his many friends, had organised a birthday party for his wife and so there we were seated with the couples as a couple. He had no kids but my being a single mother of one was no deal-breaker to him. They all looked rich, they smelled rich and spoke rich English. He was rumoured to be a member of a famous football family, one he neither confirmed nor denied. Ayew was rich, I'm talking phone by the toilet rich. I concluded on my peasantry after we dropped by his Adenta residence for him to make a change of clothes. He had spilt his crisp white shirt with red wine. "I can't go to Peter's house like this, come on Marg, let's go make a quick change before we carry on with the rest of our evening's pleasure." There was a way about how we spoke which always hypnotised me. The way he called my name "Marg" flowed with a kind of sophistication I admired. His charisma endeared me and in those moments it became known, that my heart had gone to be with this man.

It felt right when he proposed marriage within our second year of dating. It was after a painful stillbirth we had. We were beyond ecstatic when Ayew and I became pregnant. We decided to not share the news with our respective families till delivery. Eight months later, I would feel a blinding pain in my abdomen which would land me at the emergency ward of the Ridge Hospital. I was in labour. Our son was a stillbirth, we lost him. I had preeclampsia in pregnancy and somehow, that had affected my baby. The doctor said it was a miracle that I had lived. I did not know what to feel, whether to exhale that my baby had died instead of me or to allow myself stew in a bowl of depression, I felt many things.

We drove to Ankaase to see my parents. Mama had been informed so she joined Papa and my siblings to introduce my new man. Everything looked right, or so it had appeared. After that visit, Kwame and I would go our separate ways. When I met Kwame two years after the devastating break-up, he was married. He had settled with an ex-girlfriend and had held their wedding in France. He then explained the reason behind his sudden termination of our relationship. After Papa had engaged him in a talk of "Knowing me, Knowing you," he was called aside by Mama to the back of the house while I eased myself into the bathroom. He said that my Mum had urged him to not proceed with our marriage because I was a prostitute. To back her claims, she had invited Maa Yaa and Afumaa into the conversation and they supported her claims with false instances. One was that, it was the reason my previous marriage failed.

"WHAT?" I exclaimed. "And you believed them? How could you not have trusted me enough to tell me?" The feeling was beyond hurt.

He explained that he did not want to create a stir among my family members and also, he didn't believe that one's close relatives would be cruel to spew fallacies about their own. I could not believe it. Mama? Alice? Maa Yaa? How could they? What would provoke my mother to initiate a false rumour with my husband-to-be? *Ah*! My heart ached. They failed me, my family failed me. I confronted all three of them, and you guessed it… they denied their deeds and blamed it all on Ayew. I blocked all contacts of communication with my family for the next three months. Then Papa pleaded with me to let go and not cast away my family for their mistakes. Mistakes? How convenient. It was more like an intentional thought to churn nonsense and slander my image. However, as soft as I was, I let it go. Somehow, I managed to convince myself that it was

Ayew who sought a way out of what we shared. I brought myself to believe that it was the only way to not hate my family or beat myself up too much about the occurrence. After all, no one would see a good thing coming into the family and decide to scare it away.

Yemi was swift to process Akosua's visa application. He was the man delegated by Dauda to aid us with the paperwork. In about two months, the verdict came in; her Schengen visa was approved and mine was denied. Well, I did put in an application as well. It wasn't the initial plan but once Yemi threw in some words of encouragement, I thought "Why not?" All hope wasn't lost. Before Akosua's departure, we hatched a detailed plan, in which she would find an older white man, get him to marry her, get her residency permit and throw me an invitation to apply for a visa. It seemed feasible but later Akosua would indeed get married to a white man, obtain her residency and forget me and our elaborate plan for the next decade.

Family… right?

I stayed for two more years in Lagos before returning to Accra. We had lost Nkechi to maternal mortality and Berima, her husband, had returned to Ghana a childless widower. It was their first pregnancy after three years of marriage. Shola had fled Nigeria to the United Kingdom for greener pastures; Busola the cloth seller lost her life to high cholesterol Ehiziojie got married and I still taught English Language at the Salvation Cluster of Schools. Life was different, everything was different. I couldn't make new friends because I failed to get over the loss of the old. And so I returned to Ghana a few notes richer but without a husband.

Chapter 9
Becoming the other Mrs. Owusu

September 23rd 1993, Ohemaa arrived. Healthy and hearty was our daughter. She favoured her father more than she did me, with her plain forehead, heavy head and full nose. That little girl stole my heart at the first cry. To think that we could have lost her in an oversight made me love her even more. Nana Ohemaa Owusu was a chubby one; she ate, slept during the day and kept me up all night. I looked into her eyes and I could tell how assertive and strong she would be. My little one was going to be a star.

Upon my return from Lagos, I relocated to Taifa-Norway, close to Daavi junction. Taifa was one of the developing new suburbs of Accra at the time, and the greenery of the area had lured me into renting a one-bedroom in a compound house. The year was 1992; I had turned thirty-eight and was still unmarried. Kofi, my ex-husband, was re-married and bore four more children in addition to Kojo Boadu, our son. I continued to ply my trade in second-hand clothing at Kantamanto, soon, I regained my old customers and won over new ones, including superstars like Obrafour, a pioneer of Ghana's rap and Hip life music. He had patronized bed sheets from me on separate occasions. He had started his with signature dreadlocks at the time and wasn't as hot as he would become on the 2000s scene. I continued to support and take care of my family, including my older sisters and Maa Yaa's children; sending money, clothes and goodies at intervals throughout the year. I lived for the "God bless yous" whether they were genuine or not. To see my people smile, mattered more to me than anything else. Today, I look back on those memories and all I see is a young woman still trying hard to fit in with people who didn't even want her. Do I regret being a benefactor to my family? Of course not, my regret is being what I was to them from a place of fear with a desperation to fit in. Would they have wrecked my marriage plans with Kwame Ayew if they truly meant well for me? Sadly, it wouldn't be the worst thing they would do to me, for what is to come would leave your mouth agape.

Alexander Kwame Owusu was a marketing officer at the National Trust Holding Company (NTHC) in Accra. He stopped me in my tracks on one of my many weekend commutes home from Kantamanto with his 1990 Opel Kadett. He was much shorter than what I was used to. However, his dark skin had a beautiful sheen to it and his teeth - oh those well-arranged sets - you could tell they were cavity-free. His words flowed with a certain confidence, one of a man who knew exactly what he wanted. After minutes of persuasion, I agreed to have him drop me off at Taifa junction. He lived at Teshie but was en route to Asamankese, where his parents resided, for the weekend and since he would be using the Accra-Kumasi road, it made sense to hop in and drop off at the suggested junction. On the forty-five-minute drive, I would learn that Owusu was not only married but had seven children. Five with his wife and the other two from a pre-marital affair he had in his twenties. This man was ten years my senior yet nothing was condescending in the manner he interacted with me. I had not the slightest clue what endeared him to me, but somehow, I caught myself laughing at his dry jokes and wanting to stay longer in the vehicle with him. We promised to see each other again over drinks in a quieter place.

In June 1992, Owusu and I were officially involved romantically. It was about three months into our relationship and things appeared to be going well. I made a bold move this time to not have sexual intercourse with him. He objected at first but with time, he leaned towards the idea. In his words, "I love a challenge. Honestly, it's getting too easy out there of late." My decision to abstain from sex for a while seemed to excite him into wanting me more. I still could not fathom what had kept me around even after knowing he was married to someone else. Owusu had his ways of keeping a woman wanting more. Those early days of our relationship were the fondest memories I had of him.

In August 1992, we embarked on a journey to Ankaase to see my family. I think I was unconsciously warming up to the unspoken idea of becoming a second wife. Papa was bedridden with an ailment we did not know of. I believed it was the fragility of old age; it caught up badly with Papa. Some people say the amount of stress one accumulates in his youth, manifests in old age. That's what happened with Papa. My village needed no reason to throw a dance. It wasn't Christmas but the atmosphere sure did feel as such. At almost every corner someone had speakers out playing music. And in those corners were about fifteen to twenty people, chatting and dancing. The village was growing. Mama had returned to Ankaase, not to rekindle a relationship with my father but to escape the stress of paying rent in old age. Ransford also thought it was a great idea to have her live closer to her children and grandchildren now that she was advanced in age. That's why he drove from Accra to Jejeti to help her relocate to Ankaase.

After introducing Owusu as my suitor, I walked him to Maame Paulina's house where he would be staying for the two days we intended to stay at the village. He knew one or two people in Ankaase so I didn't have to worry about babysitting. I joined a few old acquaintances and primary schoolmates at the dance, catching up and wriggling our tiny waists to good music. While I was there, Mama and Maa Yaa encouraged Alice Afumaa to go and see Owusu. They were convinced, in their world, that he was the one for her. Owusu and I had agreed not to stay together in the same room during the visit so I was unaware of all the plotting and planning that went on behind my back. They took Alice to see him under the cover of darkness for the private introduction. They tried to convince him to marry her instead of me. Not only because she was my senior but because they thought that Alice complimented him more than he did me.

They had sex. Yes, Owusu slept with her. He confessed on the journey back to Accra. I couldn't believe it. He further narrated everything Mama and my sisters had told him.

"*Eii,*" I exclaimed.

"Yeah, from all this, it's safe to say that your family does not like you as much as you make them appear to."

"After sleeping with my sister, you dare preach to me about 'like'? Don't you have shame? How long was I even gone?" I sobbed.

"Look I'm sorry Yaa. Forgive me."

The words of Kwame Ayew came rushing to me. I was distraught. The writings were clear on the wall, yet, I refused to read them. A life without family would be lonely and I certainly knew that I wasn't ready to live a life apart from them. I wasn't going to allow a man to come between me and mine. The awareness of my ticking biological clock encouraged me to forgive him. That was how far I had fallen. The air reeked of desperation around me. Till today, Ransford can't seem to fathom who benefitted from the amorous relationship. Was it I or Owusu?

"Sister, he's married. Just let him go." He'd say.

But my new stubbornness was not the kind to contend with. I still stayed though fully aware that it was wrong. By December of 1992, we had somewhat settled in as a couple. He supported me financially when needed and continued all efforts towards making me his. In that festive season, we finally shared a bed and our bodies. That was when Ohemaa was conceived. Owusu visited my family again. This time, it was to pay my bride price. He presented what was requested of him and officially became second to his first wife. I didn't want to birth our child out of wedlock. But what would ensue between us years later, would render the act ineffectual.

The more I pushed the more the umbilical cord tightened around my baby's neck. When her head was pushed out, her face was already turning blue. The more I pushed, the more the blue hue appeared. The Midwife was terrified. She practised in a small space at Taifa Norway, and she came highly recommended by some people, including Adomah, the wife of a pioneer of the National Democratic Congress (NNDC) political party in Ghana, whom I was neighbours with. When Ohemaa fully came out, the midwife quickly released her neck from the cord. She blew into her mouth and spanked her bottom five times. Her eyes remained shut, her mouth also without a cry. She broke into tension sweats. After repeating the act four times. My baby let out a loud cry. An air of relief swept over the room. My child was alive.

"This one should be called Ohemaa Yaa." She suggested after cleaning up the birthing table. The Yaa was because she was born on Thursday but the Ohemaa, I wasn't too sure of.

"Why?"

"Because she has fought her way through to life."

"Yes, Ohemaa. I like that. My child is already a fighter."

"It may interest you to know that I saw this child of yours in a dream just last night."

"Really?" I shifted in bed with Ohemaa sucking aggressively at my nipples.

"Yes, I stood under an orange tree with a child and dark figures appeared from nowhere and attempted to snatch the baby from me. It was like a tug-of-war. They pulled by her legs and I by the waist. In the end, I emerged victorious and then, they fled the scene as though being pursued."

"*Awurade*! You don't say!"

"I do say, my sister. Looking at her face it felt like I had already met this child that's why I panicked when she wouldn't breathe. I had a responsibility to her and I feel I've accomplished it."

"My village is called Ankaase, which translates to Under the Orange tree. So the Orange tree in your dream.."

" *ahah!* Now it makes sense, Eiiii, Awurade ye ooo, God is good." she exclaimed.

"All the time my sister. God bless you for helping us out."

Chapter 10

Here's to single parenting!

By the time Ohemaa was Three our marriage had gone a little sour. He spent less time with us and more time with his other wife. I shouldn't have been that surprised, that's what you get for settling with a man already taken by another. The painful part was that I had come to fall in love with this man, and every minute away from him felt like an eternity. We got pregnant again. Ohemaa was going to have a sibling. My excitement was curtailed by the thoughts of my husband's unavailability. I wondered how I was going to get through this one by myself.

Ohemaa was enrolled at Shalom International School, within the *Kristo Asafo* area. I had happened to befriend the proprietor of the school before she officially opened to the public. It was one of the many private schools sprouting like mushrooms in Taifa. It competed keenly with Care Plan School, Star of the East School and Green Hill. We called her Ma - the proprietor of the school. I learnt that she had spent most of her years in America, where she had all her children, and was about to settle into retirement. I thought she looked too young to be in the retirement age bracket, but it was the fact. She was beautiful. Her light skin indeed had an American glow to it. She started in her house, where she allocated some space, including her front porch to accommodate Nursery and Kindergarten children. By the time the first Kindergarten students graduated, the building for the primary to Junior Secondary School, Now Junior High School was halfway done. However, it was habitable enough and accommodated the students and their new teachers. Ma changed the name from Shalom International School to Shalom School Complex. Janet Yeboah was one of the few friends I had made in Taifa. With her qualifications, I introduced her to Ma and urged her to install her as the headmistress for the fast-growing school. Weeks later, Janet was given the position of the new headmistress. I shared in her excitement and wished her well. Jane did me proud. Ma spoke highly of her and her deeds at the office and so did Ohemaa. They spoke of her eloquence even at a tender age. Though she stuttered a little in her speech, it could not stop her from exhibiting her knowledge and fluency in the Queen's language.

She stuttered like her father. Yes, she took after her father with that. As annoying as it was every minute with my daughter, who reminded me of the man who wasn't taking full responsibility for her. "It has to go," I thought silently, "This stammering will make life unbearable for my daughter should she grow with this." I was raising a daughter in a critical society, that spared no flaw from mockery. With her already being shy and quick to coil back into her shell, I knew I had to drastic measures to phase out the stammering before she matured into a lady. And

I did. I yelled and scolded it out of her. Whenever she did and I raised my voice, she'd pause in her breath and share her thoughts word for word. Slow and steady, a rod and another, we eliminated the stammer.

My second pregnancy with Owusu was high-risk. type II diabetes had set in at the beginning of the pregnancy and introduced several symptoms in my body. No matter how much I tried to eat well, my sugar levels skyrocketed and so did my blood pressure, they called it pre-eclampsia. I registered for ante-natal at the Ridge Hospital in Accra which was closer to my place of work. At lunchtime, I would drag my body to the hospital to sit with the many other protruding bellies. Everyone who smiled as they walked past the ante-natal unit I believed thought one thing – that these women were seated with evidence of having had sexual intercourse. I giggled to myself with that funny notion and enjoyed my own company till the ninety minutes were exhausted.

Juggling my business, my toddler, my home and the pregnancy took a toll on me. I grew weaker and started having nose bleeds and leg pain. Owusu's chicken change for upkeep wasn't enough to cover bills, Ohemaa's fees and all the ante-natal sessions and medications. I woke up in the middle of the night in the third trimester in a pool of blood. "*Ah,* God! My baby!" I cried. My legs quivered, and heart palpitations and anxious sweats took over my body. With the last strength in me, I walked to the next door to summon neighbours. *Wofa* Yaw, my neighbour, who was a taxi driver, carried me to his car and instructed his wife to look after Ohemaa. Ohemaa still slept the night away in her innocence, oblivious to what her mummy was going through.

October 9th 1996, Kissi was livid upon receiving the news. He was traumatized at the thought of coming too close to losing me a second time. While he delivered a stern warning against any future attempts at conception, the nurses brought in Obaapa, my second daughter. She weighed a healthy seven pounds. Obaapa neither favoured me nor her father as a baby. Her skin and thick hair were as golden as the sun. Perhaps the only thing which screamed my husband was her toes; all wide and oval shaped like his. My brother struggled to conceal his smile. "This is a unique one sister. She's beautiful."

I could barely sit up to breastfeed my child. The caesarian operation made it impossible to do so. The sudden hollowed feel in my middle section was disorienting. That aside, the wearing off of the anaesthesia brought me to the face of pain. So the supportive nurses fed her with some type of formula for about the first week. My husband, when he came to visit, could not accept as true that he had fathered this child. That girl was adorned with a certain kind of graceful beauty that he believed his genes were incapable of producing.

"As for this kind of child *dier*, I have never brought forth before. Are you sure she's mine?" asked Owusu. He had to be joking, I thought.

"Are you calling me unfaithful? This is a rather senseless question to be asking a woman who just emerged from a caesarian operation. Do you think I'm capable of giving myself to another man outside this so-called marriage? You had best be joking."

"Oh Yaa, relax with the words. It was merely a joke – you see, it is when you use words like so-called which awakens unnecessary anger."

"A joke? How convenient! You can't salvage the situation after spewing out what you just did. You already sullied the moment so don't try to pin it on me."

Just then, the doctor walked in on our bickering. Ours was a four-in-a-single-maternal ward. So the other patients had a field day from the many scenes my husband and I created. Save for the woman farthest from my bed and closest to the glossy blue wall. Philomena could not be bothered by the happenings at the ward for she had troubles of her own. Trapped in a world of her misery, Philomena had walked into the Ridge Hospital in Accra expecting to deliver twins – a boy and a girl. She unfortunately lost the boy due to unexpected complications and only had her daughter. The problem was her husband; he could not hide his displeasure and ungratefulness towards having a living baby girl. He had stormed out the day before from the ward after hurling out abusive words at the barely recovering mother, as though, it was her fault that they lost the boy - the boy he needed. My heart went out to her.

That night I heard her sobs. She quizzed the heavens, her gaze fixed on the white-washed ceiling. "*Awurade boa me,* help me God." she cried. "Only you are God. I'm not above you to curtail misfortunes. This one, oh, this one is beyond me." Her gasps for air in between sobs were weak. I had wished at that moment to possess some supernal abilities; One capable of alleviating her pain or resurrecting her son. They had tried over the decade of their marriage for a son but to no avail. Her husband's obsession for a son had resulted in five daughters and three miscarriages. Philomena would later check herself out of the hospital after five lonely days, filled with short visits from her oldest daughter and sister only. On her last day, she was alone, with neither a friend nor family in company. In her Caesarian stitches, she held her daughter in one arm, her bag in another and flashed a weak smile at the rest of us.

Chapter 11

The Devil is a liar

"The devil is a liar!" I shouted. It was an instant rebuke of the doctor's report. "My child will live a long healthy life. She will live to see her children's children. I was a staunch Christian at the time, but I believed that words only took effect when spoken or received with complete acceptance. Also, I knew of evil forces and I believed they were all around us - eager to grab on and implement negative words against the faint in faith.

We had been informed of Obaapa's health condition. My newborn had somehow developed diabetes. I knew I had it. It had reared its head after all the accumulated relationship, financial, emotional and physical stress I had been through. The symptoms were there, but I paid no heed. My sugar levels were high during this pregnancy. Gestational diabetes came with this pregnancy. Obaapa was prone to other health conditions as a result of the many complications associated with gestational diabetes. The words that followed nearly stopped my heart. He concluded that it would be a miracle if my baby made it past age sixteen.

I should have foreseen the arrival of such news because Dr. Adjabeng who attended to us was not too friendly. I should have seen through the many pleasantries that there was nothing good flowing out towards us after walking in on us in our usual bickering.

"Ah! I can tell you're recovering your strength." Dr. Adjabeng had earlier said, smiling ear-to-ear at Owusu and me.

"*Aane o* I feel better by God's grace. Hopefully, I get to be discharged soon." I responded.

"Oh that's good, that's good."

Little did we know that behind that plastic grin was horrible news. My husband said nothing. He gazed at the cemented floor, his right hand on his waist as his left hand wrapped around the bed rails. The tapping sounds his foot made rhymed with the sorrowful steuping sounds his mouth made. I knew for a fact that he had regretted passing those remarks about our daughter's paternity. When Dr Adjabeng exited the ward, we vowed to keep it a secret and to never tell a soul, even if that soul was family.

I said quietly to myself, "I am not empowering evil forces with this one. *Won mo eti*, they have failed." I turned to stare at my daughter, innocently asleep in her crib.

It was two years after I had my Obaapa. Back then and even now, the view has always been stunning. Staring straight at the point where skies met the ocean constantly sent my mind in awe of He who had created this. I did not count the scientific explanation of creation with all the Big Bang theory as fact. I believed there was a Supreme Being who called it all forth from nothing. Never mind, the view at the Labadi Beach resort always gets me on a roll.

I needed a breather; a break away from the usual schedules of either being at home or at the Kantamanto second-hand market, plying my trade. Afumaa had come for Obaapa to spend the Easter holidays with the family at Ankaase when she was a year old. Papa had passed away, leaving Mama and my sisters behind in the Village. He died in June of 1993, three months before I birthed Ohemaa. I believe I took the blow harder than the rest of the family. He died at age eighty-six. A life well lived. Though they lived together in the same house, Mama's unwillingness to give the marriage another try left them with a level of friendship - the good kind which saw no internal strife. Papa's death, I believe, created a deep void. One I was unable to fill till I departed this world.

My little time at the beach was suddenly interrupted by the thought that Owusu was coming home that day. Barefooted, I walked in the tickling sand to make my way to the taxi rank at the entrance. My five-year-old daughter, Ohemaa, still lived with me at Taifa. We relocated from Awonye's residence to Aunty Yaa's house close to Gech, all within the Taifa community. My husband still visited twice or thrice a month. Yes, we got "visited." He still lived with his first wife at Teshie and continued to treat ours like an affair. My children and I were the "other family." I ran out of excuses to give my rather intelligent daughter who constantly enquired about the whereabouts of her Dada.

Ohemaa was obsessed with her father. Those big eyes of hers would light up whenever Owusu walked through the netted trap door. She'd hug and hold on tightly to his legs and would let go. Then she would aim for his right hand, the one which always carried the black plastic bag which contained the meat pies and Fanyogo. They were her favourite and my husband made that a constant in her life, as if, to make up for his absence. The next thing she looked out for, away from the snacks, was a copy of the Junior Graphic. That newspaper to five-year-old Ohemaa was the Bible.

Owusu, since his encounter with my sister, stopped being a fan of my family. He did not attempt to conceal his displeasure for sending our Obaapa to the village to be with, in his words, 'Afumaa of all people.' Her willingness to share a bed with Owusu and the sneaky attempt to talk him out of marrying me was enough proof to Owusu that she wasn't in my boat. He reminded me, time without number, that, *not all blood is family.* And two years later, I went back for my child. My God had she changed! Her hair had somehow darkened and had her skin. And she looked like me now, a young me. Her little pointy nose stuck out of her face, and her full thick lips opened up to reveal a beautiful diastema. Her toes and nails stilled screamed Owusu yet; my daughter had grown so beautifully. My only concern was reintroducing her to her older sister. But those two immediately hit it off. They slept and played 'restaurant' together with empty cans. I loved to see it.

My son visited from time to time. We had become estranged. When we did meet they were short moments filled with heavy awkward silences. The space created between us by time, my voyages and ambitions proved difficult to bride. The sixteen-year age gap between him and Obaapa did not permit the two to build a healthy sibling relationship. Half of the time, my daughters could not recall who he was. Kojo Boadu only came around for my contribution towards his education, some vacation allowance or the other. He had gained entry into the Apam Secondary School and preparations were ongoing to tick off every item in the school's prospectus and those on his pencil-written ***'list of provisions.'*** He still lived with my ex-husband and his new wife, Vida - who found the bond between Kofi and me threatening. We share a son and had some good times in our marriage, so of course we had to maintain a healthy friendship. Vida was always gutted by my visits and how Kofi always offered to walk me to the roadside for a taxi. I saw her eyes twitch one time when Kofi offered to drive me to the bus station one time. Looking back, I wish I had earlier informed her of my disinterest in her husband before she pounced on me. In my defence, I was blindsided. And she on the other hand was just intimidated by my presence in her home. It took some neighbours in their Bubiashie home to dissolve the scuffle. I couldn't hide my shock. It was the last I ever stepped foot in that house. All attempts from Kofi to apologise and resolve the situation fell on deaf ears. I said to him, *"When my son needs me, let him come to me. I am done with the unnecessary nonsense. Tell your wife that I do not want you."* The operator at the **God is King** Communicatio**n Center** surely had something to chat about with his friends that perhaps, this woman had been trying to steal someone's husband. But truthfully, I couldn't care less at that moment. I needed to set the records straight with Kofi and his new love.

At the time, Mobile phones had not yet made their way into our world, so we relied heavily on telephone centres to make and receive phone calls. Whenever a call came for me, the operator would dispatch someone or run over to my house to fetch me. I became a regular at the call centre - spilling and sharing everything touching business, family, love and loss

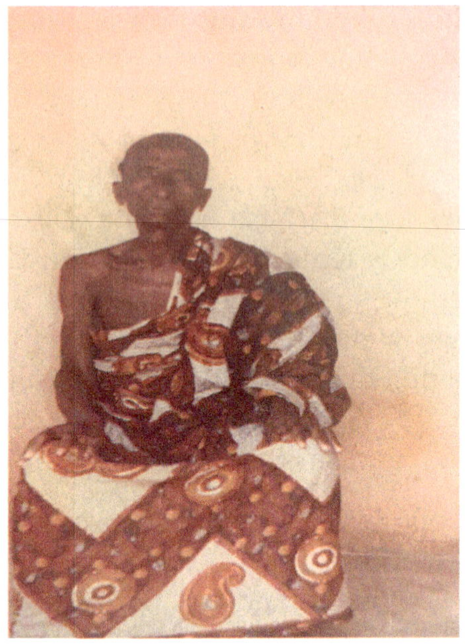

My father, Opanyin Charles Kwame Appiah-Asare Nelson, in his latter years, wrapped in one of his favorite *ntoma* pieces on his front porch at the new Ankaase.

One from the lost files; an old (almost ghostly) photo of my mother [above], Maame Sarah 'Saara' Nyarko, somewhere in Ankaase.

The three circled men were siblings. Extreme left is Kwaku Amponsah, the eldest, behind him is Kwaku Kumah, the youngest of the brothers, and the other one is Kwame Piesare, my father, captured with the Presbyterian catechist and the church elders.

Maame was a devout member of the Presbyterian Women's fellowship in our village, where all six of her children were baptized.

Ahah! Here's the mango tree where the villagers gathered beneath the moonlight to listen to my father tell his many tales. In this shot, two families held a thanksgiving service to celebrate their union.

Matriculation 1982, University of Ghana, Legon. My brother, Ransford Kissi Appiah (left) with his roommate, Alex Osei Agyekum, in freshman poses at the Annex B of Legon Hall.

The benevolent Stephen Asare, number four of the Asare bunch and my other favorite brother, a people's person he was; eager to lend a helping a hand. I never quite understood his demise.

That's me, at the front door of my second Taifa residence. I recall being obsessed with this particular fabric because it blended well with my skin tone. I wasn't wrong.

Isn't it quite obvious, that I flaunted my wedding ring from my first marriage in this shot? Ha! This was in the late 70s, somewhere on the legon campus with my co-tenant from Bubiashe, Yaw Addo. Yaw hailed from Abompe, one of the many villages surrounding Ankaase.

Mary (left), one of the grandchildren of my father's sister, Darkoa, and I at her nephew's naming ceremony at my Taifa residence.

Alexander Kwame Owusu, my second husband and father of my two daughters, in his days as a marketing officer at the NTHC.

Ohemaa's first day at Shalom school Complex, Taifa, in her first pair sneakers.

Owusu with Ohemaa, pictured on his motorcycle at Awonye's house, Taifa.

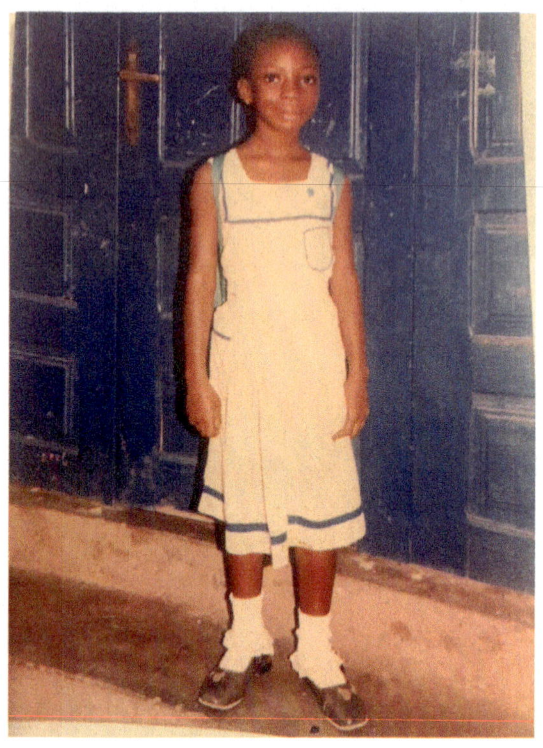

Obaapa adored her Glorich school uniform. This was her in primary six at Akweteman Zongo, Mr. Debonso's house. In view is the signature blue door of the landlord's one-storey section.

Bra George and his wife Auntie Georgina (co-tenants at Mr. Debonso's house) photographed with me (right), at the blessing ceremony of their new born at the Akweteman Pentecost church. I was given the honor to pray and speak good tidings over their daughter, Nana.

Pictured with Amelia Kande, the wife of Bra victory (all co-tenants at Mr. Debonso's house), who turned her matrimonial living room into a movie zone for my daughters and all other kids who occupied our vast compound house. This photo, though captured at a memorable wedding ceremony at Achimota Presby church, would end up zoomed-in for my obituary post.

Three of us who held spoons in this photo, except for Maa Afia (second left); already passed on into the Afterlife by 2012, from complications of Type II diabetes...Chilling! We all traded at the famous Kantamanto market in Accra.

My not-so-little brother, Kissi, pictured at the doorstep of his Taifa residence in 2023. He is the only living sibling of the Asare bunch, healthy and hearty.

A daughter beholding her first love, a mother beholding the man of her choice. I do not recall what made Ohemaa turn to her Dada in the same manner as me in this 1994 shot. Owusu and I shared in common, our love for collecting memories. This picture seemed to have captured that

My son, Kojo Boadu, then in his early thirties, photographed at a corporate event.

A penciled portrait ordered by my daughters for my grand-children in my honor. Yes, I have two grand-daughters now; one with a neck and nose like mine.

Chapter 12
Akweteman Zongo

Raising my daughters in Akweteman-Achimota was the biggest challenge of my motherhood. At ages seven and four, my daughters had to readjust to a life in a new crowded and noisy environment. Unlike Taifa, Akweteman buzzed with one occasion or the other. Every week, it was either an *Awure* or a street dance party. If it were an *Awure,* we witness days of music and feasting till the Muslim wedding was over. It took four out of the seven days we were granted a week to complete this process.

Akweteman, the small town in the Okai Kwei North Municipal District of the Greater Accra Region, would become a home for me and my girls for the next eight years. We inhabited the Zongo community together with the Hausas and Gas, both of whom were the dominating ethnic groups in the Zongo - the trenches, as the urbanites would say.

We lived in the nice part of Zongo; in Mr. Debonso's house, a wide majestic compound which in the early 2000s announced its wealth. From the second junction to the left of the Living God School, it could not be missed. Its wide blue gate stood prominent among the gateless grey buildings. Its entrance; hemmed by concrete floors, and a *Waakye* and Hausa *koko* kiosk, made it an ideal spot for the "area boys" to reassemble themselves after the day's end. A large metallic hollow tunnel, abandoned next to the *waakye* joint by an unethical contractor years prior, was the watering hole for the boys - they ate, drank and chatted evenings away.

Akweteman had a few good schools. Among these were Living God Preparatory School, A.M.A Catholic School, Glorich School and Ebenezer Preparatory School. Obaapa being the last born had to be enrolled closer to home, so, with my undying interest in the quality of Education afforded my kids, I took time to slither through the premises of the A-list Zongo School, to ascertain the one which best suited my somewhat high expectations. And Glorich School was just that.

Founded by Ms. Gloria and her partner Richard four years before our relocation, the school had marked its spot in the academic history of Akweteman. I acknowledged how my neighbour, Auntie Georgina's daughter, Agyeiwaa, rattled through the English language with flair at only three years old. I wanted that for my daughter, Obaapa, too.

It wasn't long before I went shopping at Akua's shed at Kantamanto for plain blue and yellow fabrics - as were the uniform colours of Glorich. Akua was my closest acquaintance at Kantamanto; we looked out for each other and connected on subjects away from our shared interest in the trade.

Later, she would show up at my funeral, where the greatest embarrassment of her life would be meted to her. Yes, my sisters, from their mistrust, blamed her for my death. And their reason? I would never know.

At the Zongo, I worried for Ohemaa, my oldest, who was much older and accustomed to a quieter life with simple routines, which mapped home - school - watch cartoons - sleep - repeat. The only times she exhibited signs of over-excitement were the moments her father walked through the trap-door with her favourite snacks and newspaper. In his absence, she coiled back into her shell and said less to me. I worried for her. In my worry, I went hard on her. I would scold, give her chores, and set her up to study some more after school just to get some activities running in the house. I noticed some changes in her home social skills, the attempts proved positive after all. Obaapa on the other was beyond excited. That girl enjoyed making friends with the neighbours' kids and joining them to explore the dancing grounds of some *Awure.* I caught her one time, when she was six years old, on the dance floor of one of the many Muslim weddings; as generous as the guests were, they showered her with some cedi notes and loud cheers. My embarrassment was profound. But that money, somehow, became useful at dinner time.

When we moved to the Zongo, my health slowly deteriorated. The type II diabetes lingered, throwing me into unexpected stints of fatigue from time to time. The kind the mind could not fathom - the crippling kind which set you into a brain fog and made you a shadow of yourself. Rest was advised, but I knew it was a luxury I couldn't afford. We received fewer visits from my husband and little to no contribution towards the children's education or upkeep. Oh, I worried even more! As an ailing single mother, rest was a luxury I could unfortunately not afford. However, I would later come to learn that stress was an accelerating factor for Diabetes. The one, thing which quickened my steps to the grave - stress!

No child should have to have to experience living with an overworked mother in the absence of a father. I saw what it did to my girls. It denied them a blissful childhood and affected their sense of self-worth, especially my first daughter. The incessant quest for external validation darkened her early teenage years and heightened her social awkwardness. Looking back, I have come to know that, the absence of one or both parents in a child's life has a way of disrupting the process of positive reception of oneself.

Standing on the front porch of our rented chamber-and-hall on MMrDebonso's compound, I perceived how she struggled to fit in with the other children. And once she felt an acceptance, she went above and beyond to maintain close relations with them. It was what made her laugh hard and smile more - the welcoming atmosphere lulled her into a sense of security and acceptance. *"If this would make her sulk less and grant her the kind of childhood she wanted, then I'll leave her be,"* I thought silently. And I did.

Ohemaa was given the space to navigate and feel her emotions with and away from her friends without smothering. When her heart broke from petty arguments, I did not interfere. She had developed an abandonment issue; one which I believe was created the night Owusu packed all he owned, including his newspapers and never returned.

. . .

"You do not expect me to cater for the children on my own, do you? Because it's beginning to look like I conceived them on my own without a man." I asked Owusu. My sharp voice pierced the quiet floating night. In the heat of that moment, I could care less about who among my nosy neighbours was awake to pry.

"I don't care Owusu. I won't keep my voice down. Why do I have to keep making excuses for your failure at fathering our daughters? My dwindling health makes it no fun to ply the trade I once excelled at. My debtors are on my tail, Obaapa has arrears in fees. Don't we matter to you?"

"Maggie, you need to calm down and listen to me. I'm almost going on retirement. My other children equally have arrears in fees at the tertiary level. It hasn't been easy."

"Ah! Owusu, are you saying it's all on me?"

I do not recall much of what happened afterwards. But I remember blacking out in fury when those words slipped out of my mouth. The next thing I heard was Ohemaa's cry, calling out to her Dada to stay, and when he wouldn't look back amidst all my shouting fuelled by words I can't even recall. She held onto the legs of her father and said, "Take me with you." I can't begin to imagine the puncture to her little heart ... her very first heartbreak and initiation to feeling unwanted. The desperation in her words instantly drew my attention. Had I failed my children?

Chapter 13

New neighbors, sudden deaths

Mr. Debonso had four daughters, two of whom resided with him in his two-storey section of the vast compound. He had two sons, Papa Nii and Tetteh who also inhabited his residence. His then on-again-off-again wife, Maa Lydia, would occasionally check in with her family on weekends or for some weeks. Theirs was a relationship the tenants could not wrap their heads around. Their marriage-themed the bedtime chitchats for all who occupied their residence, due to their open scuffles, they left little to our imagination. I did not derive pleasure from the stories about Mr. Debonso's role in the fallout. The circulating tales preached him unfaithful. So, imagine my disgust when this man gathered the audacity to express his romantic affection for me.

There I was, a single mother of two with a 'non-existent' marriage staring into the jaundiced eyes of a sexagenarian whose marriage hung by a thread. Rage gradually welled up within me, but at the same time, I felt sorry for him. Sorry that the desperation to fill a void had walked him to my door to request an audience. I gently declined the offer to fill Maa Lydia's shoes and sent him away with a white envelope containing my water bill for that month. With a heavy awkward gait, he walked out of the door and paused when he saw Ataa Maame, my neighbor to the right.

"Good evening, *Wo kunu aba*?" He enquired at the moment in an attempt to ease the tension and transform the questionable eyes peering at him.

"My husband hasn't returned *Efiewura;* he should be back in an hour or two. You know how *trotro* drivers stay longer in town on weekends… this is a business day for him."

"Ah! Yes yes, I know. He's a hard worker that man. Anyway, do tell him that I asked him. Auntie Maggie just gave me her water bill so tell him to bring yours when he returns."

"Alright Mr. Debonso, I'll certainly inform him."

"Okay then, *Mo nna yie wai*?"

"*Yoo Efiewura*, Good night." We responded in accord.

Auntie Maggie - it was how I was addressed in the neighbourhood. It was all I heard with greetings in tow whenever I managed to get out of bed, ignoring all diabetic symptoms. Those days, I'd throw on my African print ensemble with my signature dark red lipstick and head out to the bus station close to the Al-Rayan clinic to board one bound for Kantamanto. Auntie Maggie - it would become the Alias boldly written beneath my name on my obituary post. It was for those who hadn't set sights on me in years, those I had positively impacted in my Fifty-nine short years on earth to know that I was no more.

Ataa Maame had moved into Mr Debonso's house with her husband and four children from Prestea. Ohemaa and Obaapa were ten and seven years old respectively at the time. Like every other Rural-Urban Migrant, they had come to the city with high hopes for a better life. She introduced herself over our shared wall overlooking each other's porch, the night of their arrival. It was how I came to know about their migration status.

About a month after their relocation to Akweteman, she approached with a request to learn a trade so she could make ends meet. I encouraged her to get into second-hand trading because, with dedication, she would be earning millions of cedis in no time. It wasn't lost on me the millions one could fetch from the trade if pursued with resilience and all necessary tips and tricks efficiently applied. I knew this because *obroni wawu* business gave me my first million, but as I grew sicker and weaker, I could no longer work as hard as I did. *Obroni wawu* implied a dead white man. As children, we learnt that clothing and bedding shipped from overseas belonged to the deceased white people and that sometimes, the clothes were stripped off their backs before cremation and sent down to Africa. Hence the popular trade name … *Obroni wawu.*

I had no savings and lived from hand-to-mouth with my children with the majority of my earnings going into the accounts of hospitals and covering my children's fees. So when Ataa Maame came to me for trade advice, I saw my former self in her – a strong young woman, able and ready to give her family a better life. On the plus side, she still had her husband by her side so I knew that in no time, she would be well off.

She went with me to my shed one Saturday morning, there; I thought her skills of the trade. What to do when you're running at a loss, the best bail suppliers at the market and even introduced her to Susu collectors as a sister about to get into the business. Rolling with me at the market for twelve hours granted her the credibility she needed and soon, she was accepted by their fellow traders, even Akua.

My instincts were right! That woman was one devoted worker. I saw her life transform right before my very eyes. Her fashion sense became impressive. Ataa Maame even grew a liking for wearing lip gloss. In about four years, I overheard her discussing with her husband over dinner on their front porch about acquiring land. I was instantly proud of her. It soothed my heart that another had succeeded in the trade. Though my health diminished greatly, she became my symbol of hope. That one day, I too will rise healthily again to give my children a better life. *"Owusu would be very ashamed."* I quietly thought.

No one expected things to take a horrendous turn for Ataa Maame and her family. It threw all the neighbours in shock and despair. We worried for her and Ataa Papa's children.

2004, four years before Ohemaa sat for the Basic Education Certificate Examination (BECE). She had particularly been drawn to Georgina Ataa, the first and only daughter of Ataa Maame and her husband, because of their closeness in age. Ataa was an industrious and brilliant girl who supported her mother in her trade occasionally. Ohemaa and Ataa even came up with an idea to save as much as they could from their pocket money, to buy their own Christmas clothes. The two purchased a wooden box to keep their *susu* business afloat. Ataa Papa had bought himself a Daewoo Tico car from his earnings as a *trotro* driver, to commence his Taxi business. Things were looking good for the family until Ataa Maame fell under the weather.

It happened suddenly one Friday morning when she failed to exit their chamber-and-hall unit to bid her usual shouts of farewell greetings to the rest of us. Our porches were connected - all seven units of it - hers being the first on the left wing. It was subsequently followed by mine, then Auntie Georgina's, Brother Ernest's, Mr Adjebeng's, Mama Bernice and Amaria Kande's. As was the unspoken ritual at the compound house, we all had our morning chit-chats over the walls while making breakfast to send our kids off to school before we departed for our various endeavours Auntie Georgina's husband, Bra George the photographer, would set the dial of his radio on the local FM station. There was never a time he failed to blast the popular political morning show to theme our discussion each morning. Ataa Maame with her usual, *"nti Ghana paaa,* would we ever recover economically? Our leaders have failed us. *ohh daabi daabi!"* was enough to set the ball rolling. Brother Ernest from his porch would aggressively lament how the Kuffour Administration promised many things but was already a failure. Mr Adjabeng thought that the history of governance in Ghana was a tale of "who is who of political nonsense," Mama Bernice constantly supported his comments. Aunty Georgina played the saviour of the government with a certain assurance that things were on the verge of transforming for the better, *"bebiaa besesa,* everything would change. Very soon, you'd all gather here to hand me my stone."

That morning, I knew something was amiss. All four children of Ataa Maame wore a gloomy appearance. Three of them said their goodbyes and headed out for school but Ataa stayed home. Even Ataa Papa was downcast. He didn't say much to the rest of us as he drove the taxi out of the compound; he left out his *"okay anwumere oo"* phrase in his farewell. He only said Good morning and drove off. She cooked herbs, boiled water, and warmed some leftover soup as she went in and out of the room.

"Wo Maame wo he?" I asked.

"She's not feeling well at all Auntie Maggie. She's unable to eat or drink anything." The rest of the neighbours looked on inquisitively. Bra George rushed inside to reduce the volume on his radio set.

"Eii, when did this happen?"

"Last night. She had a high temperature last night and threw up all she had eaten for the day."

"Why is she home then? Can we take her to the hospital?"

"She can barely stand on her own Auntie Maggie. My father said that he'll take her tonight if she did not find the home remedies relieving."

"*Ah* but she was okay yesterday, laughing here and there," said Auntie Georgina. We were troubled.

Her condition worsened by the evening. Her husband, in the company of her sister and two of their children, carried her to the Tesano hospital. She was stabilised with some drips and injections. Nearly thirty-sis hours on admission, the news broke. Ataa Maame was diagnosed with HIV/AIDs. Shocking! Her husband was immediately tested and he came out positive.

The truth was, that Ataa Papa had extra-marital affairs after he came into a little money from driving the taxi. He contracted the disease from one of his many concubines and infected his wife, who had been nothing but committed to their union and supportive of his ambitions. She died in the arms of her sister a year and a half later, she was only thirty-nine. Years year after her demise, Ataa Papa followed. Leaving their four children in the care of her sister, who had come to reside in a single-room self-contained at Tesano. News of the tragedy covered the Zongo like thick smoke. At every corner were whispered questions, "Is it true?" "Did you hear?" Every member of the Zongo felt entitled to the inside story.

I worried for Ataa because she was the only female of the siblings and the most intelligent. She was appointed head prefect at her school at the time of the predicament. It was the last we saw or heard of them.

Chapter 14

Poverty a disease of nature

April 2008, Ohemaa sat among the 338,292 registered to take the Basic Education Certificate Examination (BECE) in Ghana that year. This was the Exam which transitioned Junior Secondary School, now Junior High School, students into the Secondary education level.

Day and night, I watched my fifteen-year-old commit hours chugging down the many words in her textbooks. Like me, mathematics was not her forte - it was what made her sit steadily through the late nights on the front porch. She had had no quality sleep for three months leading to the examinations which made her fragile health take a nose-dive. You see, my daughter grew up contracting one illness after the other. If it wasn't malaria, it was typhoid or some kind of skin disease. I blamed it on the kind of heavy burden she bore from a young age.

From age eight, she took the commute from Akweteman to Taifa by herself. Without an escort, she would go through the gates of Mr. Debonso into the community. Under the cover of dawn, she slithered her way through the slum to Achimota bus yard for the next available bus to Taifa. The many diabetic symptoms, the most profound of them;

constant unexplainable fatigue and neuropathic pains made it impossible to walk my child to school, even the bus station. I was no longer the Auntie Maggie of the former; my latter was a complete shadow of my reverence.

Enrolled with the offspring of the comfortable in her school and growing up from an almost nothing background, she scorned the pleasures of having elaborate meals at lunch to start saving in her *susu* box – she came to value frugality, as in our case, was the reality.

There was an unspoken pressure on Ohemaa to ace the Exams. The rest of the family even grew interested in how she'd fare. After re-introducing her to them at age ten, she frequented their premises on weekends with Obaapa. Their malicious thoughts had already come to light, yet, I felt a pressing call for reconciliation – a call to disabuse their minds of whatever they have harboured against me. So I embraced the thought of socialising with our children. I was too late.

Maa Yaa, the eldest of my sisters, bore many children, spearheading the second generation of the Asare family. Ayo Afumaa, who eventually tied the knot with an aesthetically blessed teacher from Tekyiman, never brought forth. They all resided in Ankaase till Akosua Darkoa purchased land in Accra from her toils in Germany, to erect a building of her own. So whenever my daughters would leave home on the weekends, it was to visit the grandchildren of

Maa Yaa at Dome, Parakou Estates, with whom they were closer in age. The unspoken sentiments against me had unfortunately been passed down from Maa Yaa to her children, and the agenda continued. I failed to wrap my mind around the glaring awkwardness which erupted whenever I too visited them. I thought it was poverty - the disease of nature, which caused one to flee from another. Who desired to throw a banquet for a guest who brought nothing to the table?

I had strangely been stripped of my glory but my young daughters were my gleam of hope. I knew that what Obaapa would become was highly dependent on what Ohemaa would be. So with the frailest of might, I pushed Ohemaa to be better. Concealed in every shout and stern instruction was an overwhelming rush of love propelled by the desperate desires of a mother to see her child break a lingering generational curse. Though she performed exceptionally academically, I needed her to become more, perhaps, to become everything I failed to be. I can't begin to imagine the pressure she might have felt. Poverty disrupted my academic ambitions, come what may, I wasn't going to allow it to happen a second time… no, not this time.

I borrowed from everywhere and everyone to see my children through school even in Mr Debonso's house I borrowed from my neighbours An act I would come to regret later. Though middle-aged, I still carried some kind of innocence that everyone who stopped to listen cared for me. Or anyone who smiled at me was genuine. It was to an extent. A similar lesson I had failed to learn from the treatment meted out to me by my family. My lenders, many years behind me in age, mocked me. Whenever I walked past them to our shared bathroom, they failed to make subtle insinuations to make me uncomfortable. Following their wild laughter came the hurried *slap-slap* sounds of my *chalewote* flip-flops, making their way to my lonely chamber and hall. It was unbearable. *Nea ye da hↃ no, yen sei hↃ*, but I did. With my own hands and from a place of lack, I had wrecked my only place of solace with my excess borrowing. But with no savings to relocate, I had to live in the mess financial scarcity had created for me. To top that off, I was many months in rent arrears. The devils had a field day indeed!

If I were to tutor you on anything at all, it would be to never solicit support in close environs. Go as far as you can, to people you do not know if need be. For it is better to be humiliated in a strange land where no one knows you than to suffer shame in your hometown where everyone knows your name.

Thank God for my brother, Ransford who came to bear the burden of funding my children's education. My not-so-little brother had come into success. He worked as the Marketing Manager for Shelf Oil Ghana at the time before it transitioned to Total Oil. It wasn't long till he broke away to start on his own in the Oil industry. A few years later, in fellowship with some friends bearing the same interests as he, an Oil company was birthed; one which sustained him and his family till he retired. With what was left behind after crossing out his expenses, Kissi sponsored the acquisition of my monthly diabetic herbal medication, rent and the girl's tuition fees. The humiliating calls, hinging mainly on financial appeals placed to him at the end of the month, killed me. The shame was an albatross around my neck, slowly seizing my fragile breath.

His benevolence wasn't the first showered on my children. He had catered for my son, Kojo Boadu, through the final years of secondary school into the tertiary level to pursue Marketing as a major professional course. I promised it was going to be the last he would hear about financial aid. I presume you're wondering where Kojo's father was and why he was incapable of sponsoring his own son's education. Sadly, like me, he too battled diabetes. His was advanced. Assisted by a locally crafted stick, he steered himself to and fro. When he visited me at Akweteman Zongo after so many years, I couldn't bear to look at what was left of him. My first love, wincing at each step he took. What had become of us? Ohemaa and Obaapa looked on without a clue of who he was. *"This is your brother's father,"* was all I managed to sing to their itchy ears. Both looked a little bemused. They glanced first at each other, then at Kofi, then back to each other. They treated him to a nervous smile of welcome and hurried away onto the front porch to further discuss the latest revelation. On his visit, we righted the wrongs and clarified some misconceptions from the past. Apologies were said, laughter was shared, and five years down the line, he peacefully passed away, knowing that the heaviness was lit between us. I didn't think his passing would have battered my heart the way it did. Perhaps, there was, still, a fiery something undead within.

Chapter 15

Strange Losses

Our tenancy was due to elapse in two months and I was without a doubt that I no longer desired to dwell at Mr. Debonso's residence. Even if I did, there was no hope of obtaining money to cover the expected two-year renewal cost. GH₵ 420 multiplied by twenty-four months was an equation my brain wasn't prepared to do. Then, my priority was to create some level of serenity so that Ohemaa could thrive and complete her examinations without the interference of domestic stress. And she did, waking up before the cock crew under my supervision to make the commute to Taifa for the exams.

It was all jolly when final year junior secondary students all over the country dropped their pens to the final "stop work," climaxing the BECE. Victory chants on the corner of every street coupled with loud music, witnessed many graduates violently shaking their hips in obscene motions. The same could be said of students from Ebenezer School, A.M.A Roman Catholic School, Living God School, and Reeves Academy among other notables in Zongo and its surroundings.

My old leather watch struck 9 pm and my Ohemaa had still not returned from her post-exam *Jama*. Though she had earlier notified me of her and the

'Dons of Shascoplex' (it was how they labelled their 2008 year group) intent to also hit the streets, as expected, with joyous chants after the last paper, with a swift "don't wait up" as she scurried to the door in her half laced shoes, I still worried. I'm a mother, An African mother, so feeling sick with apprehension is in my design.

By the time it read 10:30 pm, she walked through the wide blue gate. The neighborhood although drenched in darkness from the general power outage, still stayed alive. Moonlight and torchlight aided visibility so many of us at Debonso's residence perched on the single-step which bordered our front porches to interact with one another. We soaked, again, into stale conversations on failed governance and unannounced power outages. Ohemaa entered faced down in a depressing gait. Her uniform was creased and soiled. She barely broke a smile.

"Good evening." She faintly greeted, still looking down at the cemented floor.

"Ayekoo oo eii, Akwaaba. Our graduate is here. How were the papers?" Amelia Kande shouted from her corner.

"They were fine Amelia."

"Oh *Mungode Allah!* We thank God. Come over tomorrow morning for your congratulatory gift."

Her face instantly lit up, "*Ah medaase* Amelia. Thank you very much."

All who sat on the compound took turns to share pieces of advice and rain praises on my daughter. Obaapa giggled and hopped hopelessly around her sister. As though to say, "Yeah that's my sister." A proud mother moment. Ohemaa's academic brilliance, by the time she was in class six, had landed her an appointment to serve as School prefect for the primary section of her school. At the Junior Secondary School, she served as class prefect from J.S.S two to three. I had high hopes for her. My little one, also, was unanimously voted school prefect in primary six. Notice the positive pattern. She followed keenly in all her sister's achievements.

Ohemaa, again in primary six, was also among the few students selected by staff to represent Shalom School on Ghana's popular children's television show, Kyekyekule, hosted by Uncle George Liang. Obaapa on the other hand, was featured on the front page of the National Junior Graphic with two other students. It was to commemorate their school's speech and prize-giving day.

But slowly and silently, I could feel my life slipping away from me. However, to see my girls excel in their education, chalking feats I could have only imagined at their age rendered me hope and a reason to cling to what was left of my time. Behind my smiles and frequent hugs were painful subliminal farewell messages. They didn't have to know that I ailed worse than I expressed. I owed them the truth except that I had to save them with a lie. They were the essence of my being after all. At that age, they needed a brave mummy, so I gave them one.

. . .

DOME PARAKOU ESTATES in 2008, boasted of some of the expensive properties in Ghana. The community is nestled on the edge of Dome, another suburb a little north of Accra. The tarred roads made my feet appear unworthy. The people were different, they oozed class and affluence. Even the air was different and songs of the morning birds were often accompanied by a softness, an effortless tune transitioning the dawn into sunrise. The settlement was linear, each street bearing its own name and style. This would be the closest I'd ever get to America, I thought.

Dome Parakou Estates was lonely. While I was surrounded by my many nieces and nephews, grand-nieces and nephews and two of my siblings, Maa Yaa and Ayo Afumaa who came and went several times a month, their company still fostered a certain hollowness.

I slept in the farthest space away from the bedrooms. In a room originally intended for a kind of regal living room. This wide space in the semi-completed building had unconsciously been made into junk storage. If a bicycle or a toy car broke down, a couch no longer served its purpose and a television malfunctioned, they were tossed there. Even old shoes and worn-out slippers made their way to the junk room. Indeed, if no one had use for the surplus from Akosua Darkoa's cargo shipment from Germany, they too, were flung there. I recall the many wheelchairs and broken freezers heaped one on another in the corner of the room.

It was behind an unwanted wooden room divider I made my bed, it was on that floor I earned some privacy to interact with my maker and find sleep if it pitied me enough to rear its peaceful head. It would be the final place in Accra where I would lay my head till my family thought it wise to send me off to Ankaase, away from my children, where I would eventually give up the ghost.

"*Ermm* there's no room for your many belongings Auntie Maggie." It was what I was told on my visit to Parakou Estates before our relocation. It was in my desperation to find us a new home before our rent tenure expired at Akweteman. Mr. Debonso's house was no longer welcoming. Ataa and her siblings had moved out to Tesano after their parents passed, Mama Bernice had packed out with her family into their own home and so had Amelia Kande. Aunty Georgina, whose husband's responsibility was to blast the evening news on Peace FM, had both relocated to a finer house twenty minutes away from Mr. Debonso's. Aunty Mavis vacated with her son, Michael and so did Doris, her mother and siblings. They too, vacated after the death and burial of their father, Mr. Johnson. Ah!

Mr. Johnson, I remember how we were both interested in the broadcasted episodes of the National Reconciliation Commission. Colour televisions were in vogue and he owned one. Yet, there were days he would come over to my hall with his wife and some other tenants in tow to watch the broadcast on my boxy black-and-white '*atikopo*' television. It was branded atikopo by the Ghanaian locals because of its protruding derriere. The devastating expression on Mrs. Johnson's face was disheartening. So, when she decided to evacuate the premises, it came as no surprise to me. I mean why would she not? She could not bear to walk the same compound she'd created dear memories with her husband. Theirs was a love I had come to admire and envy.

My *atikopo* television caught fire on a Friday afternoon. It was around the time Ama had come to live with us. Ama was the lady Afumaa had imposed on me on my visit to Ankaase after the Easter of 2005. With my daughters in the care of Aunty Gina, I departed for my village at dawn. Hmm! It marked the beginning of greater woes.

I was to return to Accra the same day, so after the family discussions and dispersal, I clutched my purse and began my goodbyes. I saw her, Ama, seated by the right-angled wall next to the metallic barrel. I didn't make much of her presence and looked away immediately. She wasn't my concern, but she was.

"Yaa Maggie, I have brought you the help you need." Afumaa broke with her piercing voice. I fail to remember her tone variations. How her voice cut through my ear drums like a needle when she needed a favour favours up to no good. How she churned a rich baritone when in conflict. Today, I wasn't sure if she needed a favour or had something up her sleeves.

"Help?" I asked, "Which help?"

"Oh! You see. You need someone to help you take care of the children in situations where you're required to stay longer at the market. Your health too, *ehn,* think about it. You need the help *ehn,* someone to help you sell your bails quickly."

"Well, you aren't all wrong. If you say so, I'll give her a try.,"

"*Ahaa*! Now you're talking. Ama *bra* ha!" She called out for her. "See her strong neck. This one can carry your wares and sell them for you with ease."

"*Yoo* mati sister. I'll take her with me on your word." I wanted to say more. but my tongue was tied. I don't know who held back my actual concerns but strangely, they were out of reach. She puppeteered me into taking a help I did not need. The air around Ama was unsettling. It terrified me a little. Her skin was a faded dark complexion, her black hair eased into a golden brown at the tips. Her scent was slightly pungent, mixed with sweat and heat.

The first few months were okay till Ama properly transitioned into the capital. Her true colours were ugly. She overpriced my goods and kept a chunk for herself. My clients complained, and when I confronted her, she was discourteous in her replies. That time, strangely, my health deteriorated at a certain speed. A painful huge boil flowered on my head which burst to emit a nauseating smell which kept well-wishers screaming their wishes by the door, lacking the audacity to rear their heads into the room. The repugnant smell would linger in the rooms for two subsequent months when the wound would completely heal.

Ama flourished. She put on a healthy weight and new clothes. Kofi Carpee, the carpenter behind the Living God school, informed me of how Ama had come in aid of his services. She fully paid for a new three and double-seater sofa to take to her village, Tekyiman, all in less than twelve months.

Strength left me every day, and the business was in a huge hole. I made more losses than profits and could no longer keep track of the accounts. Would you believe that this silver-tongued devil got me to push Ohemaa to sell second-hand bed sheets and towels on the streets if I didn't trust her that much?

"How Ma? Why? Did I do anything wrong?" she asked woefully. It all came suddenly to her. After hours of uncontrollable tears, Ohemaa did. On the streets of Akweteman, she sold kitchen towels. The Zongo boys, who knew and admired her commitment to her education, frequented her wares. The majority of whatever she sold was to the boys. After three weekends, I stopped her. I feared she would develop a liking for making money on the streets and eventually abandon her education.

Ohemaa on the Friday the *atikopo* television caught fire, left home after 8:00 am, later than she usually did. As she opened the living room doors onto the porch, she heard a voice, faintly calling out to her unplug the television. The television she had switched on earlier to watch her favourite cartoon, 'Dexter's Laboratory.' She turned to look at the television and walked away. Till today, she blames herself for the calamity which befell us. "If only I had hearkened to words of the faint voice," she would say. The bedroom door was opened that afternoon while I slept. I was recuperating from the head wound which was already making way for new hair growth. Ama had left to handle business and the girls had left for school.

"What's that burning smell?" I asked aloud, as though with the company. The melted plastic smell was asphyxiating. But, those smells were familiar in the Zongo. People liked to burn stuff with refuse. I shut my eyes once more.

"Aunty Maggie *biribi hye oo,* something is burning in your room." Aunty Gina's husband shouted, dashing into the living room. The Lord was my strength that day indeed. A new energy picked me up from the floors where I had lain into the living room. It was the television. It was in flames.

"Eii Yesu!" I exclaimed.

Brother Ernest escorted me out of the room with pails of sand and together with Aunty Gina's husband, they quenched the fire. When they brought out what was left of the television, my heart broke. I would never come into enough money to afford a television for the remainder of my years. Ama would not join us at our next residence. I wouldn't have allowed it even if she wanted to. With all she had amassed, she packed out of the house without the decency to bid a proper farewell. Like a thief, she slithered out the of house into a rickety Kia truck which carried her newly made couch and a wardrobe. It parked at the Living God School junction, waiting for her. It was the last we heard or smelled of her.

Chapter 16

Confrontations and clarity

I run my fingers over the wooden surface, rubbing my fingers up and down. I sat reveling in the warmth of what was left of him in the seat. There was still some love there, somewhere deep inside. I broke a faint smile with tears in my eyes and my thoughts consumed by what had come of the meeting with him. My smile, full of unspoken words, and restrained feelings screamed in my head. I missed him.

Owusu had visited us at Akosua Darkoa's Parakou Estates residence. It would be his first and only visit. The last time I would lay eyes on his full dark face till I succumbed to death. In the absence of financial resources, Obaapa had to defer her education for a year. While her peers gleefully rolled in for their first term, she sadly stayed back home. Owusu had dropped by because I called. A desperate call on the Nokia 6100 Darkoa that had shipped to Ghana the same year, to supwith the payment of Ohemaa's fees, had carried him from his home in Teshie to Parakou that fateful scorching Saturday. Akosua Darkoa had brought in a variety of Nokia and Motorola phones. All of which she shared among the household, even the kids. An act I would continue to commend her for.

He was without his car or motorcycle. He had sold his motorcycle to erase a certain debt but the car – well, the car had exhausted its cycle. It had over-served its purpose. My husband, if I should address him as so, wore a khaki-coloured two-piece, comprising a loose pair of trousers and an oversized shirt, which made him appear quite stubby. He looked neat; his hair kempt in a neat afro, glittering with scattered silvery strands. The scent he wore was undeniable, the very Saturday night powder I had introduced to him in the early days of our relationship.

"Ohemaa, wo Papa aba o, come and greet your father and come with Obaa," I called out.

The girls came running, and even two of my nieces joined out of curiosity to meet the infamous man who walked out on his children. They, daughters fetched their father a wooden stool and a sachet of water. I caught beaming with a smile, one which expressed satisfaction. Satisfied that those two he had deserted under the care of an ailing mother looked well taken care of. I had not noticed the striking resemblance between Ohemaa and her father until they stood side-by-side. It was undeniable! Even in their gestures and expressions. For reasons unbeknownst to me, my heart sank again. Yet, I held back my tears, braving the emotional situation. They were happy to see their Dada after nearly a decade and I wouldn't ruin the moment with any reaction.

Owusu sat directly across from me. Staring into my eyes and looking away the next. It was how we sat when we ate together, him on a wooden stool, I on another across the separating wooden table. I recalled how he ate my fufu and *Kotodwe* soup with such gusto. "Ohemaa will soon begin her studies in Secondary School." I started, breaking the thick ice which quickly formed between us.

"Ah yes yes, you mentioned." He replied with an awkward grin.

"The schools are out and she was allotted her first choice, Okuapemman School. She had seven 1s in all subjects except for Twi, Mathematics and Pre-technical Skills where she scored 2 in each."

"Eii, she was able to score two in Mathematics?"

"Well don't act too surprised, that girl put in a lot of study hours into this exam."

"I recall her Math phobia. She would freak out whenever we presented her with Math problems."

"It's interesting to hear that you do recall the little things."

"Of course! Why wouldn't I? She is, after all my daughter."

"It wouldn't hurt to show up once in a while to establish that." I chided. A long pause. "It would be nice to give them a feel of your light as a father."

"Maggie let's not do this, at least not today." I went silent. Not much was said afterwards. We sat staring at the terrazzo floor, the both of us, feeling the heat of repressed emotions.

"So what do we do? We need to raise the required amount to cover her fees and items on her prospectus."

"Oh, she's already gone for the prospectus?" He asked

"Yes, she has, she did on her return from Yaa Tawiah's house at Tantra Hills."

"Tawiah allowed her to visit?"

"Owusu, she took her in as a help immediately we moved here from Akweteman. It felt at the moment, as though it was a condition for our stay in this house. Maa Yaa called to enforce that. She ensured it happened within the first month of our relocation."

"Hmm, Yaa, I don't like this…"

"We didn't have a choice, Owusu," I said almost in tears. "We had nowhere else to go. I couldn't bear another two years' advance cost. It's not like you're forthcoming financially." I continued, "She threw her out anyway."

"Eii, yet you deem them as a family? Ah, Maggie!"

I saw his eyes redden. My report filled him with indignation. I wondered why he didn't play hero at that moment; carry us out of this house, away from these people into a new space. Something held him back, and it wouldn't come to light till the weekend he stood beside my well-adorned corpse laid in state. It was the day I would see him cry for the very first time - the day he would recount every bit of financial humiliation he had suffered in the time our children were of age. I heard him, even wept with him. I wanted to tell him it was all okay and that I had already cast that aside. I apologised for the treatment meted out to him at my funeral and encouraged him to go and wrap our daughters in an embrace, yet he heard me not. That day I saw love again, in his cataract-infested eyes.

Owusu left behind a sealed white 'Eno Serwaa' envelope, holding his contribution to Ohemaa's admission expenses. My legs failed to carry me to walk him to the gate, so the girls did. I thought I deserved a "thank you" or a "well done" for holding the fort in his absence. I was tired. Impoverished motherhood exhausted me. A hug would have sufficed but he flashed a weak smile as mine, and said, "I'll let you know when I safely arrive at Teshie."

Already disappointed by the lightness of the envelope, which I knew contained nothing substantial, I sat back on the wooden stool to plot and plan, sadly, my next line of action - Where and who else to turn to obtain some funds for Ohemaa's education. Owusu had left me Two hundred Cedis to pay for part of the school fees. We were required to pay a total of Eight hundred cedis to the School's bursar by the first week of October. By the time of his visit, it was August 10th of 2008, leaving me with two months only to cover everything and sort out uniforms for my daughter. When her mates would reach out to her on my phone to enquire about her preparations, she came out with a story, well-oiled with lies they easily bought into. Even I did, at certain times, escape our reality for the brief period of her pithy narrations.

I barely had a wink of sleep that night. My body ached, my heart raced, and my palm sweated from the failure of my brain to come up with a concise image of what next to do. Ransford had made it clear that he was no more funding my children's education. After seeing Ohemaa through junior secondary school, he was done. He too had a family to cater for and I blamed him not. Kojo Boadu had not been gainfully employed after completing his marketing course. It had been years and he still had nothing to show for his many years of education. I knew better than to ask him because he too struggled to fend for himself. I cried.

Pozo was one of the few people I met in my heydays at Kantamanto. His was a moniker given due to his mobility disability, the difficult gait of a man whose left leg bent inwardly towards the right. He too sold and hawked, in the years past, bed sheets and towels at the market. We had managed to keep in touch over the years, so, when I phoned him the next morning about my being in limbo; he suggested that I come over to his new shop at Lapaz. The electronic dealership was his new line of business. He bought, shipped and sold televisions, laptops, kettles and air conditioners. Everyone knew and loved him on the Abeka road. It was he who suggested that we pursue a scholarship from Rev. Sam Korankye Ankrah at the Royal House Chapel. It was where Pozo worshiped and he believed that if my children and I followed him to church the Sunday of the same week I had visited, to see the Secretary of the scheme; we were likely to the considered. He walked me to the bus station after stylishly sneaking a hundred Cedis into my purse. Again, I cried, all the way home on the bus.

The queue at the Royal House Chapel Secretariat was extended almost to the main entrance. After sitting through hours of a full service, I was famished. My body shook slightly, I grew weaker by the minute and anxiety swept in, as was with diabetes. Obaapa, with the offertory she had concealed, walked to a local Yoghurt seller to get me Fanyogo and meat pie. I devoured them in minutes. Rising with a new energy, we made our way towards the last person in line. Hours flew by, sunshine made way for the moon and we had only made it halfway in the queue. "Mama let's go home, you are tired. Besides, we can try again next week." Ohemaa suggested.

"And what if we do not get the money needed to cover transportation for the three of us to come all the way here?"

"Mama God will provide. He always does." Obaapa chipped in.

We exited the premises and made way for the Circle bus station to board a Dome-bound bus.

"Mama let's buy *kenkey* and fish when we get to Dome crossing for dinner before we starve tonight." Said Ohemaa

"*Ahh* yes, we should. Because I'm not sure that we would be left any portion of whatever they decided to cook today." Ohemaa consented.

They had a point. You see, the dynamics at Parakou were such that, one held the power to decide who was served and who was not. It was not so at the beginning. Doris, the partner of Kofi Gyasi, the second son of Maa Yaa ran the kitchen in the home. I say partner because, after nearly two decades of being together, he had failed to make the union official, so in their late thirties, they cohabitated. I, at one point, approached Kofi Gyasi and encouraged him to take her to the altar. "You owe to your children to bestow honour on this woman and her family," I advised. He failed to heed my counsel. When we first moved in, and Ohemaa was sent away to slave for Yaa Tawiah for two months, She included Obaapa and me in her meals. When I came into any amount, regardless of however meagre, I would quickly surrender a portion as my contribution for food shopping. It continued that way until the money stopped coming and Ohemaa moved back in with us. Her responses to me were curt and so were her daughter's. A poor man indeed has no friends. Yet I didn't blame her. She only bent to the will of her sister and mother-in-law. They, after all, were the ones who wielded the power to make her an official wife. I felt sorry for her.

The next Sunday at the Secretariat was even worse. Hundreds of parents, mostly mothers paraded their children at the front office. They all, like me, helplessly sought means to get their wards enrolled in school. By twilight, we had only made it halfway as the week before. "Mama, by the time our case would be heard, classes would have already begun. Please let's not make more stressful the state we're in. We'll figure something out." It was what Ohemaa said that made me walk out of the premises that very evening, never to return.

Chapter 17

At their mercy

It was Pozo's idea that Ohemaa ventured into hawking sachet water to raise funds for school. He said he would top up with whatever would be left to cover the total expenses. On August 29th 2008, he purchased her, a yellow plastic bowl to use in the new endeavour. My daughter believed it impossible to raise all we needed in less than two months. Additionally, she did not want to go back to hawking. "Mama, are saying that there's no alternative? Must I do this? What if we never raise the money and I end up a street girl or a girlfriend to a drugged-up ghetto boy?"

"God forbid it! It won't happen. Pozo said it will work and we all need to embrace optimism at this point. My God is not asleep."

Oh yes! My faith in God was alive. I had deepened our friendship in the days I suffered the mysterious head boil and He forsook me not. On my Bible, each night, I lay and prayed, to the one I knew would come through for me. I trusted Him. I couldn't see how yet I believed strongly that He would.

After spending two days trying to dissuade me, Ohemaa finally decided to ply this trade.

"Mama let me go with her," Obaapa said. "We'll keep each other company. It's not like any of my cousins would entertain me if I stayed back. so let me go with her. We'll sell faster."

"Okay. Ohemaa please keep watch over her on the main road. Hold on firmly to her at all times, please. You two should watch out for the buses o. those *tro-tro* drivers are lunatics on the road."

"Okay, Mama." Only Obaapa responded. Ohemaa still directed her frustrations at me… as she should.

I nurtured thoughts of going to Yaa Tawiah's house to bawl my eyes out. She had, during the days Ohemaa lived with her, mentioned that her husband had an interest in her education. I was desperate. I planned to go and kneel before her to reconsider offering their support but later in the day, I shoved it somewhere at the back of my brain, where unpleasant memories went.

The phone call from Maa Yaa was rather brief. When her name popped up on my phone's screen, I had assumed it was to be a courtesy call, a sister checking in on another. So when she opened with, "Now that you're at Parakou, do all you need to do to not step on toes or irritate anybody. Ensure to do all you can to help in the house and live in harmony with them all," I was taken aback. It didn't end there, she concluded with, "Tell Ohemaa to pack and leave for Tantra Hill. You know, Yaa Tawiah just had a baby and she would need the help. Now that Ohemaa is fresh out of JSS and has nothing to do, let her go and help around the house." We weren't offered a choice, it was as though, all was discussed and decided for us without prior notice. I would later come to learn that, it was Darkoa who had called from Germany to say that her house was overcrowded and that, she neither wanted me nor my children there, especially Ohemaa, and her offence? I would never know. This, I believe, was Maa Yaa's way of helping out; making us demonstrate our desperation for shelter using service.

Her first night in Yaa Tawiah and her husband's house wasn't all bad. Ohemaa would narrate how she was served a plate of rice with egg stew. She said Abena Linda was there too, in all her half-welcoming choral greeting. They whispered to each other lines of family gossip, making her uncertain of her stay. There was no proper induction whatsoever, Ohemaa was left to figure things out for herself as time progressed. Theirs was a rather spacious chamber-and-hall with a kitchen and an open area adjacent to their building, designated for a dry line and *fufu* pounding. They had a little walkway leading from the bedroom into the hall, it was where Ohemaa kept her clothes. "You can place your bag here," Yaa Tawiah pointed later that evening, "It was where Dzifa kept her suitcase so you can leave yours there." Dzifa was the help Maa Yaa had deployed from Ankaase for her daughter. She lasted less than two years with Yaa. Dzifa abandoned her employers a sunny Saturday afternoon after Yaa had left for her shop, leaving behind a crumpled note with hectic lines of misspelt words. They however communicated her message, that she had had enough of the daily cumbersome tasks. It was obvious that she watched too many Nigerian movies.

Ohemaa made her bed in the heart of the angle where the two gigantic sofas met. She found it cosy - cosier than the storage room I made mine. Each morning, she was required to rise before 6:00 am to get water boiling for her husband Agyei and first son Gabby. Gabby, their two-year-old was already enrolled at Rockies International School. A school made for the haves which sat at the pinnacle of Tantra hill. She was to walk the entire fifteen minutes to the school with Gabby on her hip and walk back. At 3:00 pm, she was to walk back to the school to fetch him and make that walk with him on her hip or her back. When she felt like it, Yaa would allocate some cash for a taxi on return.

Her younger son, Junior, was very much a baby. She only bathed, fed the little one and made him ready to go with his mother to the shop. Ohemaa was then expected to sweep the vast compound and living room and clean the kitchen, bathroom and toilet. Then she would wash dishes, and clothes and cook. On some days, she was expected to show up at Yaa's tailoring shop after the many chores to sit around till Yaa thought it was late enough to close up. On some days she forgot to eat. Every chore was left hanging around her neck. If she failed to do them, there would be a minute talk of how lazy she had become. "I'm not a machine," she would silently murmur.

The subsequent days grew tedious with tasks, unchanged, and unadjusted. The landlord, who occupied the other of the two buildings on the compound, had a son, Jeliu. They practised Islam and barely familiarised themselves with their tenants, save for Jeliu. He drew closer to Ohemaa and at times, aided with the chores. On days the taps failed to run, he offered to fill Yaa's many gallons at the nearby public tap with his wheelbarrow while she did the laundry with Lil Wayne's hit song 'Lollipop' on full blast on the Television. She spoke not of Jeliu's help to Yaa and her husband. My daughter, like me, found solace in music. It was how she expressed her unspoken emotions, and how she completed her chores with ease and speed. About a month into her stay with the Agyeis, Kwesi Darko, the son of Kofi Gyasi and the first grandchild of Maa Yaa, was also sent away to live with Yaa Tawiah. I blamed Kwabena Kennedy, the half-useful son of my sister whose only drive, was to cook up stories about any member of Darkoa to curry favour. He had informed Akos about Kwesi's smoking habits at the house, which we were already clued up on. We would later come to learn that Kennedy had added some unprintable lines about Kwesi in his stories to Akos, and she, growing shallow, bought into it without enquiring from the rest of the family. He joined Ohemaa at Tantra Hills and shared in her chores. He was swift to befriend Jeliu, with whom he was closer in age. Jeliu let him borrow his wheelbarrow to cart the many gallons to the stand-pipe, eight minutes away from the house.

Then my turn came - my turn to be kicked out to join the two to find refuge at Tantra Hills. Darkoa wanted me out for an unshared reason, and so, with my bag-packed light, I too, went there, without Obaapa. She stayed behind. I saw how hard my daughter worked, even Kwesi. I saw how they took little breaks. My daughter's eye bags hung loose, as though she were middle-aged. I complained not, for I had no other means to shelter my children.

I indulged in the National lotteries during my four-day expulsion. I would send my daughter off with numbers scribbled on a piece of paper. Some single digits others double.

"Tell the man at the lotto kiosk to perm the numbers for you. Ensure he does before you pay."

"Okay, Ma. But how do I know it's been done?"

"He'll indicate it on the sheet."

With this, I'd send her off with a cedi note. 6:00 pm took longer to strike. I waited anxiously for the winning numbers to be announced on the radio. I won - seven hundred cedis. Yaa Tawiah was intrigued. She wanted in on the lotto too.

"Eiii Auntie, you should have informed me before sending Ohemaa off in the morning. Please inform me before your next stake." Yaa Tawiah remarked.

The next lottery day was Thursday. As per her request, I informed her before Ohemaa exited the premises. She too won, eight hundred cedis, as did I. She phoned her mum to share in her glee. Soon, every other member of the family was privy to the news of the lottery, even Akos. She immediately instructed Kennedy to have me return to the house. I wondered if they thought I was about to come into some fortune, so they wanted to iron things out immediately to get into my good graces. Looking back, I'm certain that their lack of education had impoverished their brain and sense of reasoning, leaving them with mediocre thoughts and assumptions.

Kwesi Darko returned to Parakou with me. After lamenting the burdensome chores to his mother, she summoned him back to Parakou. "Auntie Maggie, will be on her way tonight, make sure to come with her," Doris said, strongly.

Two weeks later, Ohemaa phoned from a call centre pleading to be released from Yaa Tawiah's house. "*Ma m'abrɛ o.*" indeed she was tired. I stayed up all night trying to figure out how to help my daughter. But as life would have its twists, Yaa Tawiah would send her packing in the middle of the night to Parakou without fare.

Her reason was that, by calling me to complain about how overworked she was, she had thrown mud on her character. But what was said when Kwesi called his mother to make a similar complaint? Nothing. She had done her a favour by accommodating her so in her defence, she had no cause to moan.

"Agyei had expressed his interest in sponsoring your Secondary education but with this attitude, he would be a fool to see it through." Yaa Tawiah said, among her many accusations of Ohemaa having an affair with Jeliu. They comprehended it not that, two educated young and sophisticated people could develop an affectionate platonic relationship. Illiteracy is indeed a disease. Ohemaa before leaving the house, informed Jeliu of what had transpired. He in turn informed his parents who did not look forward to renewing their tenancy contract.

"Ohemaa, I must confess that when Dzifa had expressed her woes to me as you, I helped her run away. I honestly thought you were the new help till you revealed your relation to them." Jeliu continued, "How could you be cousins to this woman? Unbelievable!"

"Hmm Jeliu, it's all good. let me find my way to Parakou. My mother has agreed to meet me at the bus station and walk me home. It's almost midnight."

Jeliu slipped a fifty cedi note into the left pocket of her long pleated mini skirt. "Take this for a taxi or food for your mum and sister. Keep in touch." The two would keep a healthy phone and Facebook relationship till Jeliu was sent away to America for a fresh start. It would be the last she would hear from him.

Chapter 18

Help has a source.

It was sweltering in Accra the day Ohemaa and her sister left for Lapaz. Coupled with the unexpected traffic, their hearts were laden with rue that they had opted to embark on the endeavour that day. On arrival at Pozo's shop, he redirected them to the wholesaler who supplied all sachet water hawkers at Lapaz. The store, buried behind the Tabora and Mallam station yard, was owned and operated by an overweight woman, Larley. The large room boasted of not less than ten industrial-sized freezers, in which bags of sachet water were crammed. The girls watched as some scents flew by to make deposits for their bags. Each bag, containing thirty water sachets, sold at eight cedis at the time. Selling each sachet at fifty pesewas equalled a total sale of fifteen cedis per bag: eight cedis as cost price and seven cedis as profit.

They walked on the streets, hand-in-hand, saying more to each other with their eyes than with lips. Ohemaa was blinded by her tears, moving wherever the wind went. She wanted to call out for buyers yet words failed her. She swallowed air with her saliva, slightly choking in each gulp.

"Yeeeeesss, pure water!" Obaapa cried. Looking left then to the right with each call. She knew her sister was hurting and feeling insignificant among the many ordinary hawkers who had succumbed to their fate.

The first bag sold in minutes, and so did the next and the last two. The customers, mostly young men, who were eager to mingle with the two girls who in their words "did not favor the streets," emptied their on every refill. The girls were ecstatic. They returned with twenty-eight cedi profit and some food they had bought with the bonus Pozo had given them, Ohemaa had wished it to be the last time she would hawk water, but she did the next day and the day after for almost weeks; some days with Obaapa, who was already growing attachment to what she deemed an adventure, and other days without her.

When Ohemaa walked into the mechanic yard behind the Kwashieman station, she thought it was an ordinary Friday to make sales and get some food on her way home. It saddens me to say that, she had adapted to her new life as a hawker, dashing all hopes of ever joining her mates in school.

"Ohemaa !" a voice called. It was from a moving ToyLand Cruiseriser. It was one of her colleagues who was returning from Accra Central with her parents. They were coming back from purchasing all the items on her school's prospectus. Priscilla was scheduled to check in at the St. Roses Secondary School in two weeks like all other students. When she enquired about what she was doing on the streets, Ohemaa lied that she was selling out of curiosity. She wanted to know how hawkers truly felt on the job and that it was her first and last day. Priscilla did not buy that but she feigned an agreeable smile. This daughter of mine has to be a lawyer or a writer. She had the knack for telling little white lies when the need arose.

"Write to me when you get to Okuapemman okay? I would like my friends at Roses to know that I know a brilliant one at the Great Okuas."

"Sure."

Ohemaa watched her run into her mother's four-wheeler, waving vigorously at the cloud of dust they left behind. She walked into the mechanic shop defeated. Angry even, that she had been seen hawking.

"Maame give me one." a mechanic called from beneath one of the many broken vehicles in the yard, disrupting her thoughts.

Another called for her from the neem tree which was gloriously at the centre of the enclosure. A *waakye* seller sat there with her sales girl, some workers and an older man in a white polo shirt and a black pair of jeans. He sat with the yard owner, waiting on their plates of *waakye,* gari and *wele.* He appeared ordinary. Not much to be made of him.

"*Amaria* I'd like a three cedi plate please." Ohemaa requested.

"Are you taking it away?"

"No, I'd have it right here, thanks."

She didn't know what caught the man's attention. He appeared to be gravitating towards her; asking Ohemaa why she didn't buy any protein for her meal and observing keenly how she violently swallowed the half-chewed rice and beans.

"Papa I'm saving for school o. if I keep buying expensive protein for every meal, then I may as well abort all my academic plans. *Yɛnfa anumdɛ entua school fees.*" Ohemaa replied in between scoops. It gave them quite a good laugh.

"Saving up shouldn't strip you of well-balanced meals. Amaria please give her a fish and two rolls of wele. It's on me."

"Thank you."

The man said, turning to his friend, touching him on the shoulder, "My nephew scored an aggregate of thirty-five at the BECE. His mother and I had to grease some palms to get him into Adisadel College."

"*Saaa*? I thought Jeremiah was the smart kind." the man asked, looking a little bemused.

"Oh, my friend forget about him! That boy had us all fooled with his plenty English."

"*Nsuo wura,*" He beckoned to Ohemaa, "Did you write the BECE?"

"Yes, I did."

"Aaannddd?" he asked. Everyone eagerly looked on.

"And what sir?"

"Well, what were your scores?" He asked softly yet commanding. I'm guessing this is how it'd feel to have a father around, Ohemaa thought. There was something about the way he spoke, how he leaned forward while discussing pressing issues - an undeniable fatherliness to him.

"I had Seven ones and three twos sir," Ohemaa replied standing, with one hand resting on the other behind her.

"Making an aggregate score of nine in all, am I right?'

"Yes sir."

The shock was out there. All gathered frozen for a long minute. All wondering one thing at the moment, what she was doing selling sachet water on the streets.

"What are your parents doing about your education?" The man asked, his friend nodding aggressively in agreement.

"My mum is sick, she can't do much. My sister had to drop out of school for me to complete my Junior Secondary education. She's a single mother. No one seems to be interested in sponsoring my education."

She burst into tears, it was unfamiliar and healing. It was the first time she realised how much she had bottled up on the inside. She felt lighter. She felt seen.

The man finally broke his silence, heaving a sigh.

"If my nephew, with such a horrible score, has been able to go to school, then I'll see to it that your academic expenses are covered."

"Yes Yes, *Nyame Nhyira wo.*" The others chanted the blessings of God over him in unison. Even the Amaria gave Ohemaa a pack of waakye to take home to her sister. She said it was how she was also supporting on the new academic journey, a well-nourished body.

The man then introduced himself as 'America Man'. The popular owner of the string of sawmills at Dome-Crossing. Ohemaa was shocked. She recounted admiring the vast space, teeming with workers, sawdust and wooden chips. It was at their entrance, that I donated a cedi to a beggar who kept calling out for help. She gave America Man my number and he wrote down his on a piece of cardboard paper. He promised to call later that night to arrange for a meeting with me.

I was stunned by the news the evening Ohemaa arrived. It had forced me to pee a few times. My bowels went a little loose. "Are you sure? Are you sure?" I asked twice with emphasis on the latter. I didn't want my joy to be tickled for nothing.

"Yes Ma, he said I should call him when I get home and that he doesn't want to see me ever on the streets again." She replied.

"So does this mean you'll be home a lot more now?" Obaapa asked, Clinged onto her sister.

"Haha, yes yes sister. We'll go for long walks on the white people's street."

"And around Dede Ayew's grandmother's house?"

"Yes yes, there too."

The sound of the dialling tone made me more anxious. My mind worried from the many flashing 'what ifs?' Then he answered. It was true. American Man was visiting tomorrow to discuss the way forward. I couldn't believe my ears. My God had finally heard me.

I stayed up all night praying. I read the Bible to ward sleep off, for I feared that American Man might reconsider his decision if my eyes were shut for a minute.

What seemed like ten years of waiting was finally here. It was the longest 6 pm of my entire life. He drove a white Toyota pickup truck and wore a white long-sleeved shirt paired perfectly with a pair of blue jeans that Saturday. We walked him from the gates of the Viola guest house into our home and assumed the position of Owusu on his visit. He reiterated his interest in sponsoring Ohemaa's education to any level he could while he lived.

"Her future looks promising and I would like to be a part of the story." Dearest reader, I wept as though I was in mourning. Jehovah Jireh had shown up, big time! He requested to see the prospectus, which Obaapa hurriedly fetched for him.

"Aaahhh! Okuapemman Secondary School. Great Okuas! It's a very good school. Well done Maame. You've made your mother proud." his comment unleashed another batch of tears, that of gratitude. He pushed a sealed envelope into my hands and bid us farewell.

"Inform me of the outcome of your journey to the school on Monday. That's when you'll submit the draft from the bank right?"

"No sir, I'll go to the bank on Monday and travel to Akropong to submit the drafty on Tuesday."

"Yes, that sounds reasonable."

"Okay let's keep in touch. You girls should take care of your mother."

"Yes sir." My girls shouted, smiling from ear to ear.

I knew the other occupants of the house would be curious. They knew of American Man as the rich sawmill owner who said little to strangers. He was the popular man at Dome. They all tagged him as a snooty rich man so when they saw him walk into the house with me and my children, they had wondered, but they dared not to ask.

"Jesus!" I screamed. I counted one thousand four hundred cedis. Enough to cover her fees and all enlisted on the prospectus. I quaked with shock. How could a stranger be more affectionate than one's own blood?

As the days grew closer, I grew more and more dejected for reasons unknown to me. But as she flashed that bright smile from the hired taxi to Akropong, my fears were allayed and I knew she was going to be just fine.

I recall how the other members of the household watched us carry the scanty items in the check bag and chop box. How the sincerity in their unwillingness to assist us had infuriated and saddened me. How they looked on with unaffectionate interest, whispering one to another about things they only knew. The words they lent were "Wo ne Nyame nkƆ." Indeed, she would go with God and she would emerge victorious. It was clear as day, they did not expect her to come by means to further her education. But look at God.

Chapter 19
Still as a log

Kennedy was filled with curiosity. Not the good kind which caused one to stare at the other in admiration and awe, but, the intrusive kind which poisoned the air and stifled relationships. Such was his contribution since he resurfaced from Gabon.

He who was believed to be dead after his long disappearance in the Francophone African country, appeared at the doors of his sister's Parakou Estates house in the early 2000s, with nothing but huge boxes piled with old magazines and newspapers rotting with exotic cockroaches. It was the first time I saw a white kind of bug. It was shameful. He lived for negativity - anything which called a garment of shame and despair on the other, he indulged.

He was the first to inform Obaapa of my admission to the Mahama Hospital. Not that he cared, his look of excitement masked by the feigned expression of concern gave him away. Even the corners of his mouth slightly bent upwards in contentment when Obaapa hastily dropped her backpack and dashed for the gate. She had resumed her schooling at Shalom School Complex, where her sister had graduated from. We still had no money. It was Janet, the friend I had earlier introduced to the school's proprietor, who had offered to cater for her tuition through Junior Secondary school. That's how my Obaapa sat in a classroom again.

I had suddenly craved mashed kenkey with some milk and peanuts, and Efia, the help who served Yaa Tawiah and her family, had offered to prepare it. Yaa Tawiah had unfortunately relocated to Parakou with her husband and children after Adjei suddenly lost his job. It all happened within a month after she had kicked out Ohemaa from her home.

Three taps on my shoulder and I was still unresponsive. Three harder slaps on my calves and I still lay unmoved as a log. She felt the alarming coldness of my skin and called for help. Still resting peacefully on the tiled floors of the storage room, Efia continued to impel her taps on my unyielding body while the others, including Kwabena Kennedy, called for a taxi. Maa Yaa was there at the time on one of her countless visits.

I regained consciousness after Obaapa settled into the seat adjacent to my single hospital bed. My mind boggled with the "why and how" I was at the hospital, dived into mourning. Mourning a death I had missed rather than celebrating my escape from its cold arrest. Ohemaa was away in Akropong, reading General Arts to become the journalist I was certain she had the grace for.

"Let me get the doctor. " My daughter said after noticing I was awake.

"No. Don't. I'm fine. Let me rest a while. Thank you, Jesus." I couldn't describe the feeling I felt. I felt many things, I thought many things. The words which slipped out were expressions of them all; gladness, gratitude, fear, rest, peace, confusion. The issue, I would be informed later, was with my blood sugar. It was extremely low.

I do not recall when I yanked the drip needle out of my hand, however, I did, violently, creating stained sheets as in a crime scene. I walked to the nurse's desk, where Obaapa stood, and demanded to be discharged. They called for the doctor, and after further examinations, I was free to exit the premises with a mini bag of medications. Kofi Gyasi already was by the gate in a car he operated as a taxi, to take us home. My brain still recovered from the break of life as we drove through the estates.

There would be an outpour of love and shows of concern for the next two days. After which the coldness, not of my body but of my family, returned, even more powerful than ever.

Ransford visited monthly with a stipend. The four hundred cedis he had willingly decided to give me every month. It covered my medication, food and Ohemaa's transportation to some extent. Ohemaa was home on midterms. I observed the eyes which followed us when I drew him aside to engage him on medical issues. Kennedy lingered, moving with one bucket after the other past us to the adjacent tap on the compound. I found it funny and exhausting for him. So when Ohemaa informed me of what she had sighted at the entrance of the storage room, I laughed harder.

Ransford called my mobile phone on his way to his Taifa house. Kennedy had shamelessly occupied the master bedroom in which his sister slept on her Christmas visits to Ghana, not only for the comfort of it but to also easily monitor my moves and eavesdrop on whatever conversations may transpire from that storage room, my room.

"Maa Maa, come and listen." He said in a low tone, pulling his mother, my sister to my closed door. They both assumed the gossipy posture, leaning forward with an ear resting on the door. They listened with care as Ohemaa watched from the Children's room. Ohemaa heard me too. My laughs and giggles on the mobile phone that night in 2010. They hurriedly walked away to Yaa Tawiah's room immediately after the call ended. Exchanging whispers and confused expressions.

"Ma," Ohemaa opened after saying our usual midnight prayers.

"Uhuh?"

"Are you sure Maa Yaa is your sister? *Daabi,* Are you certain of your relation to any of these people?"

"Ah, erm yes I am. What is the matter?"

"I saw Kennedy drag Maa Yaa to the door when he overheard you laughing your heart out on the phone with *Wofa* Kissi."

"The door?"

"Yes. They pressed their ears on the door and listened to every word of that call." She answered.

A deep sigh. "Well, I was only talking to your uncle Kissi about general matters and laughed when he told a joke. It was a regular sibling conversation."

"What would she have done if she had slipped and broken her hip on her way?"

"Who?"

"Maa Yaa. What if she slipped on her quest to gossip with her son?"

"I'm sure they would have blamed you for even her fall Ma." Obaapa chirped from the corner. It sent me into a laugh.

"I agree with Ohemaa Ma. I don't believe they're your relatives."

I couldn't sleep that night. I pictured the mother and son leaning against my doors and discussing away from my hearing, what they had heard. If only I had some money, I thought, I would bundle up my children and leave them be.

Pat the shop owner on white house street was fond of Obaapa. She had befriended my little girl after her many visits to her shop. She grew curious about this well-mannered girl who often came to purchase cream crackers, Milo and mosquito coils.

"They're for my mother. She's bothered by mosquitoes where she sleeps so she needs the coil." Obaapa had replied.

"And where do you sleep?" Pat asked.

"In the children's room with my sister, when she's on vacation from school, and my nieces too."

"I see."

Obaapa recounted my being plagued with diabetes. How they had nearly lost me to low blood sugar.

"How is a diabetic woman surviving on Kenkey in the morning and Milo at night? Those foods can kill her quicker you know?"

"It's what we can afford. They don't feed us in the house even though they're aware of my mother's financial woes. As and when they wished, they slipped a plate of rice or a bowl of fufu."

"Take this," Pat said, pushing a fifty cedi note into her palm. "Buy some plantain or diabetes-friendly food for your mother today."

"My mother would be upset. She doesn't like it when I tell people of our struggles."

"Tell her it was your savings then."

Obaapa couldn't tell a lie. She confessed and rushed to Dome station with her sister for cooked plantain with *Kontomire* stew and salmon for me. The two enjoyed some Kenkey with *kpanla* fish. It was the best I slept in years that night.

It was why I made my way to Pat's shop the next morning to express my gratitude.

"Auntie Maggie, you need to avoid Milo and bread. They could spike your blood sugar levels." She advised.

"My dear, I know but isn't that better than starvation?"

She introduced me to her mother, Auntie Aggie, who was also diabetic. She looked too healthy to be classified as such. We bonded right away. She got lonely at her house when her children went about their daily activities so she thought it a good idea to have me over all the time so we 'old folks can have a good time.' She was the best friend I've had in years.

Pat and her family fed us, clothed Obaapa, sold provisions to Ohemaa at highly subsidised prices for school and made me feel alive again. I no longer sat outside the gate when Obaapa went to school, I went to see Aggie. I no longer felt lonely at home with my family who had no use for me, so I went to see Aggie. Aggie, who played ludo, cooked and ate cocoyam fufu with me. Aggie was my sister, the one I had wished for. Obaapa was happy to watch the shop for Pat on weekends while she did her chores. She preferred that to sitting at home in a soup of tension, waiting on who would speak to her that day. She waited on all except for Sabatha, Kofi Gyasi's sister-in-law, who also lived and slept in the children's room. She too had been whipped with the tongue of some members of the family and understood my plight. She particularly enjoyed Ohemaa's company when she returned from school. Ohemaa would occasionally help out at the food kiosk she operated and would run light errands for her.

My new smile appeared to have bothered them. Obaapa's new weekend job had ruffled some feathers. They watched her attend to them at Pat's shop with discomfort and immediately sat to discuss among themselves. Maa Yaa called from Ankaase, where she lived with Afumaa and her husband after Mama's passing in early 2008. Yes, Mama passed away, old and feeble. She was well over ninety-eight. A long life she had that one. She was buried with the ashes of her son, my brother, Stephen Yaw Asare, who quietly passed away in Switzerland. Like everyone else, he had relocated to the European nation for greener pastures. Ransford travelled to see to his cremation and sent down his ashes to be buried along with Mama. He was the first of my parent's six children to depart to the afterlife. He was survived by three children and a wife in Ghana.

Maa Yaa had called to query me on my reason for allowing Obaapa to work at Pat's.

"If she doesn't have anything to do on weekends, why can't she wait on Yaa Tawiah? She needs the help than Pat." She fired. There was an unfurling in my stomach.

"She's gainfully employed there. I don't see an issue with that. Perhaps, if your grandchildren played with her, she wouldn't have eagerly accepted the job."

A long pause. "Well, Yaa Maggie, I still think she should be at home helping out Yaa Tawiah not Pat. I've said what I called to say." With that, the line went dead. Who tells another woman what her child can and cannot do, especially when what's being done is highly beneficial? My top went off. I was furious. Only poverty could open the door to insufferable encounters. Obaapa continued to help Pat and we continued to eat well and laugh more. My body did not experience a minute of iciness in a long time.

They thought they could collapse Pat's shop with a boycott. Majestically, they walked to Amakye's store, three minutes away from Pat's. One by one they walked past to spend their money elsewhere. When we wouldn't budge, Kwabena Kennedy turned on his rusty charmer boy effect to woo Pat. He suddenly was enamoured and frequently visited the store. His, I now believe, was to win her over and eventually make me unpopular with them. It was desperate and devious of him. Yet he failed, miserably. He too, joined the others to fly past Pat's store to Amakye's. My God liveth indeed.

Chapter 20
Taifa-Burkina

Kojo Boadu at age Thirty-two remained without a job. He continued to abide in a government flat with two of his father's children. After graduating from Apam Secondary School, where she read a three-year Marketing course in college, he was unemployed. He lived on earnings from temporal road activation gigs for commercial brands, nothing substantial to even open a savings account with. His girlfriend at the time, Nancy, supported him with her allowances. I mention Nancy in this paragraph because, when push came to shove, she became an anchor.

Akosua Darkoa, as was her trait, suddenly didn't want us in her house and this time it was aggressive. It was in February 2011 and she had made clear her plans to spend Christmas of that year in Ghana and how she did not look forward to seeing me and my daughters in her house. I had no money and little time to even search for something. Hoh! Which landlord in Accra would offer a room on credit and allow payment in instalments?

Auntie Aggie offered some amount which could only cover six months if the cost was one hundred and fifty cedis per month. My head ached. The prayer was to depart before the Easter holidays in

April. It was in the wind that she planned on dropping in earlier than the presumed Christmas.

It was a Sunday morning when Kennedy called on me, smoothly, as he did when he was up to no good. He held an envelope containing some cash Akosua had wired in aid of our moving out. "Wow, she really didn't want us here," I thought. I do not recall what had birthed her vendetta against me, but whatever it was, I had hoped for a day she would sit me down to reconcile. It never happened. Ohemaa was in the first term of her third year in Secondary school and had returned to Parakou for vacation in March. Quickly, we bundled up all we owned with the excess we kept in the storehouse of the adjacent house, *Atadwen*'s house.

They looked on, conceited, as the blue Kia pick-up truck softly swayed on the untarred road.

"Did she come to bid you farewell or to express any form of gratitude?" I heard Yaa Tawiah ask her mother, who had returned from Ankaase to await the arrival of Akosua Darkoa.

"Yes, yes, she did." Maa Yaa stood Akimbo with an expressionless face, watching the blue truck buried in the dust trail.

At that moment, it dawned on me that, I had given my family the power to tell me they didn't want me, twice. An access denied me from one generation to the other. It was a lost battle. The driver of the Kia truck flashed a smile. As though to say, I see you, you will be fine.

My eyes spoke of the unshed tears, the silent wails of my heart. I was exhausted from a seemingly unending battle between life and me. Was it too much to ask to be loved?

It was Nancy who told of my plight to her mother. They were quite comfortable; not having too much, not having too little. Her mother traded in Holland wax prints at the Georgina stores in Accra Central. She was enrolled in the finest schools in the country, her father saw to that. She loved my son, Kojo Boadu. The two had been an item for about three years at the time. Nancy's mother owned a gated semi-completed house in Taifa-Burkina. It was a three-bedroom detached house sitting on four plots of land. There was a single-room outhouse occupied by a young family of four. They too had been evicted from their former abode due to failure to pay rent. Nancy's mother had offered them the outhouse, so they could watch over her property. Four years later, they still watched over it and the house remained in its partial glory.

She was there that day, Nancy's mother, with my son, to hand over the keys to the main house. It was peaceful. A mini banana plantation hugged the house from behind; it reminded me of the village, cool and green. Nancy's mother, as with most landladies, was half welcoming. Forcing a smile with such difficulty it made the veins on her forehead pop.

"Take care of my property Auntie Maggie. I leave you with God." those were her last words after exchanging pleasantries and introducing Naomi, an occupant of the out-house to me.

At first, I gave myself three weeks. Three weeks to carry myself with whatever strength was left within, and return to Kantamanto. Someone may be kind enough to loan me some bails of clothes or sheets to sell, I thought. A month elapsed before I went to Kantamanto. Ohemaa had returned to school and Obaapa had switched from Shalom to Bethel Association School. Janet could no longer keep up with the high fees at Shalom. I was, indeed I am still grateful for her decision to solely cater for Obaapa's education. I too needed to do something to feed my children and restock my medication. At this point, the diabetes I managed poorly had begun eating away my flesh. I looked like something out of a wringer. With part of what was left of the money we had, I did go to Kantamanto. The first day was good and so was the second and third. Akua was helpful. She provided me with some sheets at highly subsidised prices to sell. Those three days were reviving. I had missed it, the busyness of rising every morning to strike healthy bargains with strangers. Then the fourth day, as I settled into my old life, forsaking all forewarnings my body had given, I regained consciousness at the shed of Awo Botchway with several people encircling. The story was I had passed out after getting off the *trotro* from Taifa. I could only recall feeling a numbing pain in my stomach and dizziness before alighting. Awo mentioned that my body had gone cold and had stiffened from the legs.

She advised, "Maggie, you shouldn't overwork yourself if you're still in recovery. The work will be here always and if you keep going like this, it won't be good. Think about your teenage girls." Of course, I thought about my girls. They were the reason I had returned to the occupation I once loved.

A man shouted something in Hausa and three men rushed to sit me up. Then two hours later, they handed me an envelope with some cash and a bag of groceries. It was a contribution they had made in my name weeks before my return.

"You are the reason most of us have come to understand and appreciate *obroni wawu* business. Take the needed break and attend to yourself." Faustina said, leading the delegation. Where words failed me, my tears said thank you. Truth was, I felt like a charity case. The once ambitious hardworking lady was now reduced to attracting pity funds. I hated that my body failed where my spirit was willing. I went home in a chartered taxi, still bawling my eyes out.

Two months later, we were back to square one. No money for food or to send Obaa off to school. I spent most of my days lying on the floor of the porch in the afternoons, sweeping at random the already tidied compound or just listening to the whispers of the wind. If I listened attentively, I could almost hear my name or someone making conversation with me about a Bible scripture I had read. The boredom was evident.

Obaa skipped class a few times. On days I had no coins to give her or when I fell seriously sick she couldn't leave me behind, it happened often. A part of me died with each day that passed, hope evaded me, and my body failed me. Returning to Kantamanto would imply that I needed more pity donations. God forbid it! It would be the last thing I'd do. Ransford would have helped if I had called on him, but he already put me on a stipend so, demanding an increment would be a huge show of ingratitude. The man had a wife and a child and I did not want to add up to his burden. Besides, when American Man disappeared suddenly after sponsoring Ohemaa for a year in school, it was Ransford who had stepped forward to pick up from where he had left off. Oh yes! He did. His sawmill folded up too. No one knew where and what had occurred. It was like he never existed. I didn't feel entitled to anything my brother earned or owned. I respected and admired how he had built himself from the ground up and acknowledged the fact that he had his world of problems as an adult.

Chapter 21

Take care

And then Obaapa begged on the streets. My thirteen-year-old daughter would on days she couldn't join her colleagues in school, walk the streets of Taifa-Burkina to beg for money. Her plea was that, her mother was ill and needed support to buy food and pay her medical bills. She spoke not of her endeavours till someone forced her to explain how she had come by a lot of food one Saturday morning.

There, I knew I failed as a mother. I was charged by God to protect and provide for her.

"It's only my fourth time Ma. I'm sorry I won't do that again. I just couldn't watch us go hungry every day. You've grown feeble and I know it's as a result of hunger and worry." She explained.

I retorted, "Let me see you go out to do that thing again, you'll tell me who between the two of us the parent." The truth was that I was ashamed, ashamed of my failure at parenting. However, we ate the Kenkey she brought home for supper that day and the day after, cooked some rice with the money she had received from her sympathisers. Those three cups of rice braised in oil and beef with a side of ground red pepper sustained us for a week. When all was done, Obaapa went out again, this time with me in tow

A man rolled down the glass of his window and spat at my feet. He assumed that I feigned helplessness. My heart broke, but we moved. With the twenty cedis we were blessed with, we filled up our barrels from the community tap and restocked some groceries. Was it better than returning to Kantamanto? No. but I thought it better to receive help from people I was likely to never see again than people who knew me. Besides, I lacked the energy needed to hustle in the market as before. I also lived with the trauma of what had been from the last time at the market. I feared another attempt would end me up at the morgue this time.

And then I went cold again. Obaapa had left to appeal for funds as usual. It was about noon when she exited the premises. I lay on a cloth on the porch on an empty stomach which rumbled at intervals. If you or a loved one has had or has type II diabetes, you know better than to miss meals. She gained nothing from the three hours spent pursuing strangers. A tap followed by another, each one more vigorous than the other still left me unresponsive. The out-house was empty so she rushed outside to appeal for funds again to get me food. She knew what happened when my blood sugar was extremely low. She panicked. With tears in her eyes, all she approached refused to help, they glorified her with one insult and another. She returned to find me in the same position, on my left side still cold, still peaceful. She went out again not knowing where she was headed. Where her legs went she obliged.

Two honks and Obaapa still did not turn. On the third, she did in a swift. It was Ransford. He was stopping by on his way from work. He too lived in Taifa. Upon hearing what was at stake, he jumped out to help her carry me into his car and he drove at a top speed to the hospital. To date, He can't seem to explain what had led him to drive by that fateful afternoon. Call it a divine intervention.

January 2012, Nancy's mother came calling with deadlines. She was ready to continue with her building project which required our moving out. I panicked. Sick and without funds, I decided to contact Maa Yaa. Even if it required that I cried and knelt, I was prepared to and I did. Akosua had returned to Germany and agreed to have us return to Parakou. I occupied my former sleeping room with my daughters till Obaapa was registered to sit for her BECE. The diabetes progressed unbeknownst to me. I had been so wrapped in my many worries about life and the well-being of children that I had paid little attention to my already deteriorated health. My kidneys and liver silently, slowly, failed; a side effect of diabetes. I no longer carried urine like normal people did. My eyes were cloudy, my gait slightly mimicked that of an alcoholic - I had lost my balance. My brain took longer to process information, than I did as a child. I gave up on ever making it in the city and decided to relocate to Ankaase without my girls.

"Promise to pay me a visit when you two are done with school," I said seated next to the bus conductor in the Anyinam bound *trotro* at St. Johns station.

"Yes, Ma." They responded in unison.

"Mate, *mepakyew*, drop her off at Osino and help her board a taxi to Ankaase." Ohemaa pleaded with the conductor.

"Sister, no worries at all. I'll see to that." said the conductor.

I was sad but I knew I had to leave. To leave to a place where food was free and conversations flowed. A place I could live rent-free and be at peace. My girls wept and so did I. It felt like a final goodbye yet, it wasn't. I was proud of myself that day. The thought, that I had single-handedly raised strong independent women, who now possessed all it took to navigate their paths, kept me at peace throughout the two-hour journey. The benevolent conductor, who only gave his name as Nsiah, carried my cloth-tied and double suitcase luggage to the booth of the yellow and green 'moving taxi' at the Osino station. He returned a part of my *trotro* transport fare to cover the taxi trip. Not that I could not afford it but he had insisted for reasons known to him to bear that cost. I was grateful. Teary-eyed, I squeezed myself into the front passenger seat, looking forward to what awaited me on my father's compound.

Maa Yaa was home with Afumaa and her husband. There were Atobrah and Korkor, the teenagers who had been wheeled off from their hometown to work as help for my sisters. They were receptive. Almost happy that I had finally succumbed to my ailments and retreated to the countryside to rest.

The countryside - it was where everyone went on retirement as if awaiting the cold hands of death to come knocking on the *wawa* doors. The countryside - it was where you settled when you had nothing more to live for, where you went when your energy residue no longer satisfied the vibrant demands of the capital. They were like shadows, all who lived in the village. Forlorn figures slouched their way through the day as shadows; here today, gone the next. Funerals were the weekend parties for what was left of the youthful population. Ankaase had changed. Illegal miners destroyed our rich farmlands and polluted the Birim River. Young ladies wore cheap 'togo' figure-hugging clothes in loud colours to entice the miners who eventually made wives of some of them and single mothers of the unfortunate many.

Ator and Korkor carried my luggage to my room and rushed to the *mukaase* to get ready my *fufu* and dried fish pepper soup for dinner. The room given to me after my brother Stephen Yaw Asare, had erected a new building next to Papa's old house, was sandwiched by sisters. Maa Yaa's to my left, Afumaa's to my right. It was a major he completed before he passed away in Switzerland. His reason was to make sure all six of Papa's children had their own rooms on our father's compound; a luxury we couldn't afford growing up. Sadly, he never got to walk the length of the house before his demise.

Then I got a bench from the carpenter at the main junction. Placed next to my door, it was on this bench that I spent my mornings, afternoons and evenings. My sisters chatted to me mostly about politics, news of who had died in the village and what had killed them when they were home. There were days when they would have their conversations which exempted me. But it was okay, I was used to that. I wasn't expecting them to feign a bond. It would have been insulting to our collective integrity.

And then Ama Mary returned from Accra. She too, like the others, had had it with the city life and craved some quiet. Her mother had sold porridge at the market square when we were children. I would spend most of my days in her house on her bench. I recounted the moments with my daughters at the bus station. She brooded with me over the well-being of my children.

"Yaa they are still young. They are still babies. How are they going to survive in that house in their absence?" She asked with much concern.

"Ama, *M'ani da Yehowa so.* I trust Him to cover my children and keep His angels charge over them. Ohemaa is done with Secondary school now and so Obaapa just wrote her BECE." I continued. Blowing my nose harder in my clothes. "They will be fine."

"Hopefully Darkoa doesn't show them to the exit out of the blue, you know, as it is with her. Hmm."

"My sister please, don't even call it into existence. I barely sleep at night with those two on my mind."

"I know. Your expressions give you away. You miss them."

"Yes, I do. Especially Obaa, my little one. I'm supposed to be with them, protect and cater for them but my failure..."

"Stop using that word Yaa!" she rebuked. "Which failure? You are the most benevolent human I've ever met in my lifetime. It is your body that failed you, not your soul. You have the desire to push harder for your children but sickness got in the way. You are not a failure."

I smiled. I agreed with her. It was the vessel that failed not the soul. I would spend five days each week in Ama's house and walk her to her backyard farm to uproot some yams. It was a good exercise for me. I craved the company too. I thought it better than the silence I was subjected to in my sisters' company. I no longer wanted to fit in with them. I was done. I only felt sorry the awakening took that long.

When Obaapa arrived in Ankaase in June 2012, the damage in my nerves had progressed. There were days I could not feel my limbs. On others, I experienced temporal memory loss which terrified me a great deal. My sisters rebuked me in the presence of my child for needing to be in the company of outsiders than theirs. I said nothing. My daughter, though only fourteen, was privy to the ways of the family. Like me, she said nothing. She would spend the next three weeks cooking, washing, and when it called for it, bathing me. She walked me to Mary's house on some days and to the roadside on other days. Ohemaa called every day to check on us. When she came into some little money, she would transfer half of her earnings to the mobile phone she purchased for me.

That red and silver Tecno phone came right on time; about a week before I departed for the village. Ohemaa worked temporarily after school as an event usher with Empire Entertainment at Laterbiorkoshie in Accra. It belonged to the famous media personality Bola Ray and one Mr. Collins. Empire was set to organise a concert where major Nigerian acts were billed to perform. I didn't understand the new school music but I recall her making a lot of noise about Davido being a main act. Ah! days before the concert, she sang and danced to his *Dami duro* and *Ekuro* noisily in my sleeping space at Parakou. That girl wasn't the best dancer but she sure can sing. My favourite memory was from the night before concert day. My daughters forced me to move my feet to Davido's music. I didn't detest that. It was a pure moment for all of us.

"Ma, why are you dancing like Michael Jackson again?" they teased.

"Isn't it better than this your choreographed leg work?"

They burst into laughter. Obaapa's being the loudest. She danced. Very well of all three of us.

We laughed and hugged and teased Ohemaa for being a lousy dancer. I was genuinely elated for the first time in a long time. With her earnings from ushering at the concert, she departed for Circle station in Accra, where she purchased the phone. Moved by the grand gesture, I spoke blessings over my children and prayed to the Lord to preserve their days.

It was on that phone Owusu called. Obaapa had texted my number to him. When it vibrated in my wrapper that afternoon, I wasn't expecting it to be him. Some nights I caught myself blaming him in my thoughts for how my life turned out with my children. Why didn't he fight for me? Am I not worth fighting for? How was it that easy to discard me? I wondered. But it wasn't all on him. Offered two choices, I opted to have him father my children. No, I don't blame him entirely. He had called to ask for forgiveness. One that I freely gave him. He had expected me to sing songs of frustration and blame. Owusu was shocked. He called every day after that and attempted to form a bond with his daughters. They still held him responsible for how I had become.

"Let it go Maa. Let it go. He is still your father. Don't let us spit our sourness into your mouth; else it will seep into

all of your relationships. It's poison. Let it go. Let us deal with our mess and live a happy life devoid of bitterness and nonsense. I only entreat you to learn from where we failed." I said that with my eyes closed, reliving pleasant memories of Owusu in my thoughts.

Ohemaa visited in August after Obaapa returned to the city to follow up with her BECE results and all the craziness associated with school placement. Ohemaa, though only eighteen, spoke like an adult. Our situation had forcibly matured my girls. She spent only a night.

"Take care of Obaapa. Take her everywhere you go. Protect and support her in any way you can."

"Okay, Ma. She's my little sister of course I'll be there for her."

"Okay, okay. When you save enough money to rent a place, please come for me. I have no joy in being in Ankaase for too long." I said, my face downcast.

"Don't worry Ma." She replied. Placing her hand over my shoulder. "I'll come for you. Then when I get more money, Obaapa and I will fly you to China. I hear those people can cure everything. So you can return home stronger and younger, even with a Chinese husband."

The thought of myself with a Chinese husband cracked me up for a long time. I repeated my request as she walked out of the house towards the main road.

"Ma do you need me to stay another night? I could inform the organiser that I wouldn't be available for the event you know." she hated to see my cry. My impenetrable eyes and sad countenance concerned her.

"No, you go. You need the gig to cater for the two of you. Go. Call me when you arrive."

She hugged me and started her walk to the main road, where the many Accra-bound sprinters plied.

Then Kojo Boadu gained employment with Ransford's Union Oil Ghana Limited. He was to manage the Enchi branch in the Western Region. That August was joyous. My son called and sent me money every day. I often forgot whereabouts in my suitcase I saved the money. The more I misplaced them, the more he replaced them. On days he visited, he would press a slender envelope into my hands and whisper,

"Keep it well Mama. It's for your medication and hospital checkups."

My son had become a big man. I encouraged him to get his sisters relocated before they were suddenly kicked out, to which he agreed. He got an apartment for himself and his future spouse in Kasoa and nurtured plans to do the same for his sisters. My heart was finally at peace. On some days, when he visited and my vision was cloudy, I could only hear my son and focus on the warped image of him my eyes painted.

Chapter 22

Lights out

THE ULULATION broke the silence of the village. The streets, teeming with men and women in black and red clothes, marched with the slowed ambulance. As it parked, the pregnant clouds gave out rain, refusing to permit the opening of the booth. The scene was confusing. Strange and familiar faces wailed in the rain. I had a growing I was adrift and isolated. I was light as air moving at varying speeds from one end to the other. Then the rains stopped. Permitting the strong men to fling open the doors of the booth. They carried a mummified being into a room and the ambulance drove away.

It was the second time I saw myself lying peacefully, The first being on the 15th of September 2012, at 1:15 pm, when my daughters on another visit, commanded a sound from me. I felt as though I was sinking into the hard cemented floors of my room. All lights dimmed until I could not see a thing any more. Then I suddenly stood over my wailing daughters, watching them watch my lifeless body. Souls can't weep, they only feel emotions. It was disorienting at first, in fact, I resisted a little bit but I eventually embraced my new reality. A reality free of pain and all the aches and weakness my body felt. I was free.

I followed Maa Yaa as she made a call to Yaa Tawiah in Parakou to break the news.

"Maggie is dead oo." She announced.

Yaa Tawiah replied, "As for her we knew she was going to die. It is vultures who would feed on her flesh."

"Eiiii," I screamed. What would provoke a person to say such a thing? How on earth did I offend this girl? Well, the good thing was that I wasn't alive to strongly feel the arrow she had sent my way. I wished her well.

What broke my heart was that I had not prepared my daughters well for the life ahead. I tried telling them that all was okay on my end but they heard not. There were, however, a few times, they applied what I yelled out to them in a moment. I continued to mother them even from my new realm.

Ohemaa joined the two men who volunteered to cart my body to the morgue. Ohemaa sat with them with my body on the thirty-minute journey to Bunso, where my body was wheeled off to the VIP section of the morgue. VIP, yes Ohemaa made sure of that, even greasing the palms of the Mortuary man to handle my remains with extra care.

The funeral was a big one. Friends I knew, colleagues I had met on my journey, mostly from far away, somehow heard of my departure and graced the Occasion. A few of them were paramount chiefs of certain towns. Our compound was filled with people, so much so that six tents had to be erected outside.

It was an open casket and I truly never looked gorgeous in a white dress. I had always wanted to wear a white flowing gown at my wedding but I couldn't. We stuck to customary proceedings, forsaking the typicality of a white Christian wedding. It didn't matter; I got to see myself in one either way. Only this time, I failed to feel the fabric on my skin.

Owusu stood perplexed by my body unsure of how to feel. Words took longer to form and make meaning for him. He rendered lines of apologies, vowing to reconcile and draw closer to our girls. I could not agree more.

Food was in excess at the occasion. Many loaded all they laid hands on into giant polythene bags, to feed their families back home. I bet they lasted for days. A scene contrary to what I had experienced in my latter years.

I spied all three of my children nestled closely beneath my father's mango tree, discussing when and how the girls would move to the rented apartment in Kasoa. Kojo had indeed fulfilled his promise. My daughters were in safe hands.

I watched Yaa Tawiah, Kennedy and Maa Yaa wail, a shocking scene my soul struggled to process. It was unclear what the true emotions behind the tears were. I learnt at that moment, the essence of directing all the energy exerted in people pleasing these, towards honouring God.

And now, notice how I pen these closing words in my own handwriting, that indeed, while men wish one to suffer alive than to have the sweet release of death, it is essential to love freely and embrace whatever lessons are thrown at you.

Printed in Great Britain
by Amazon